Neon Galax

Kristine Snodgrass & Andrew Brenza

Neon Galax

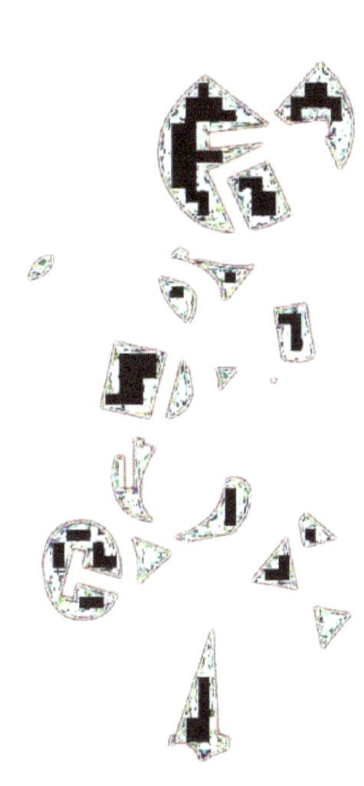

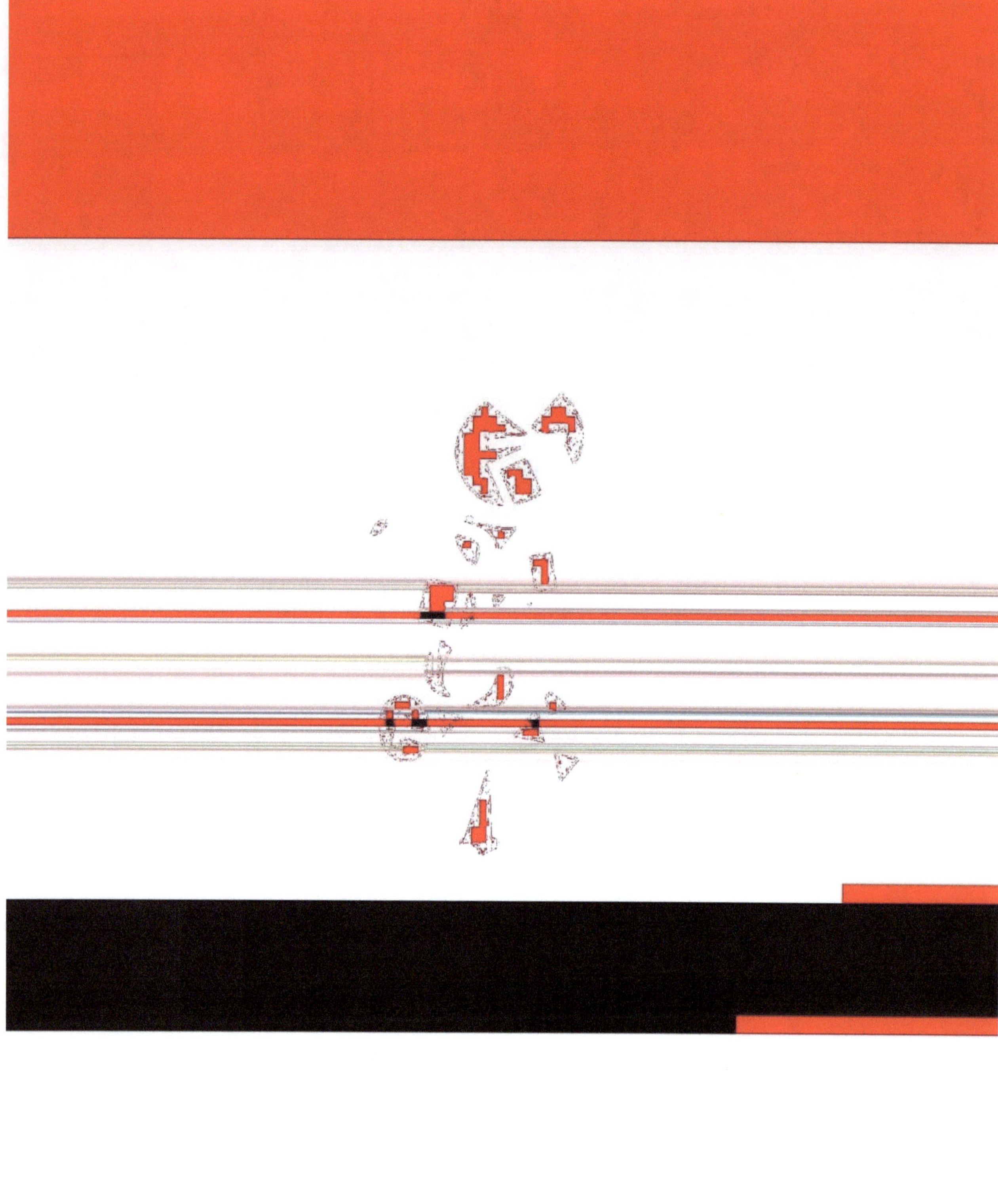

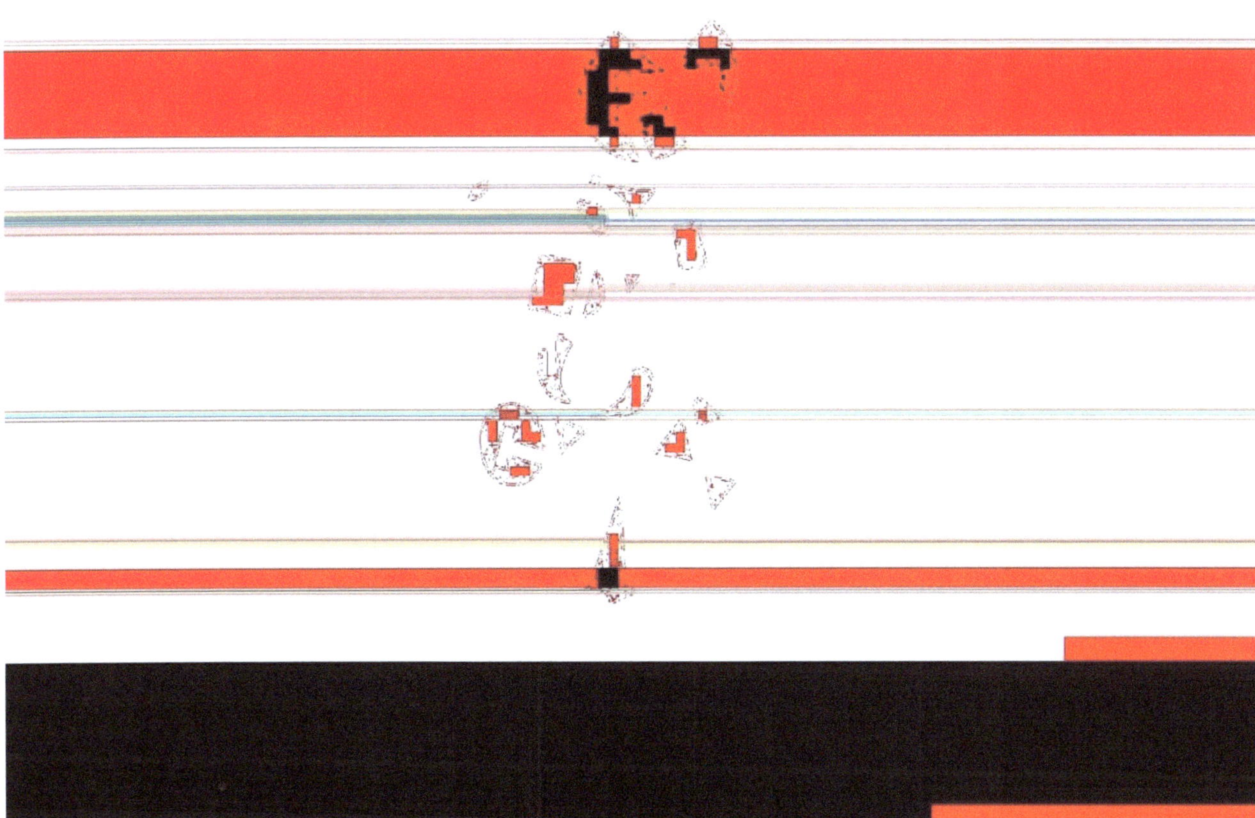

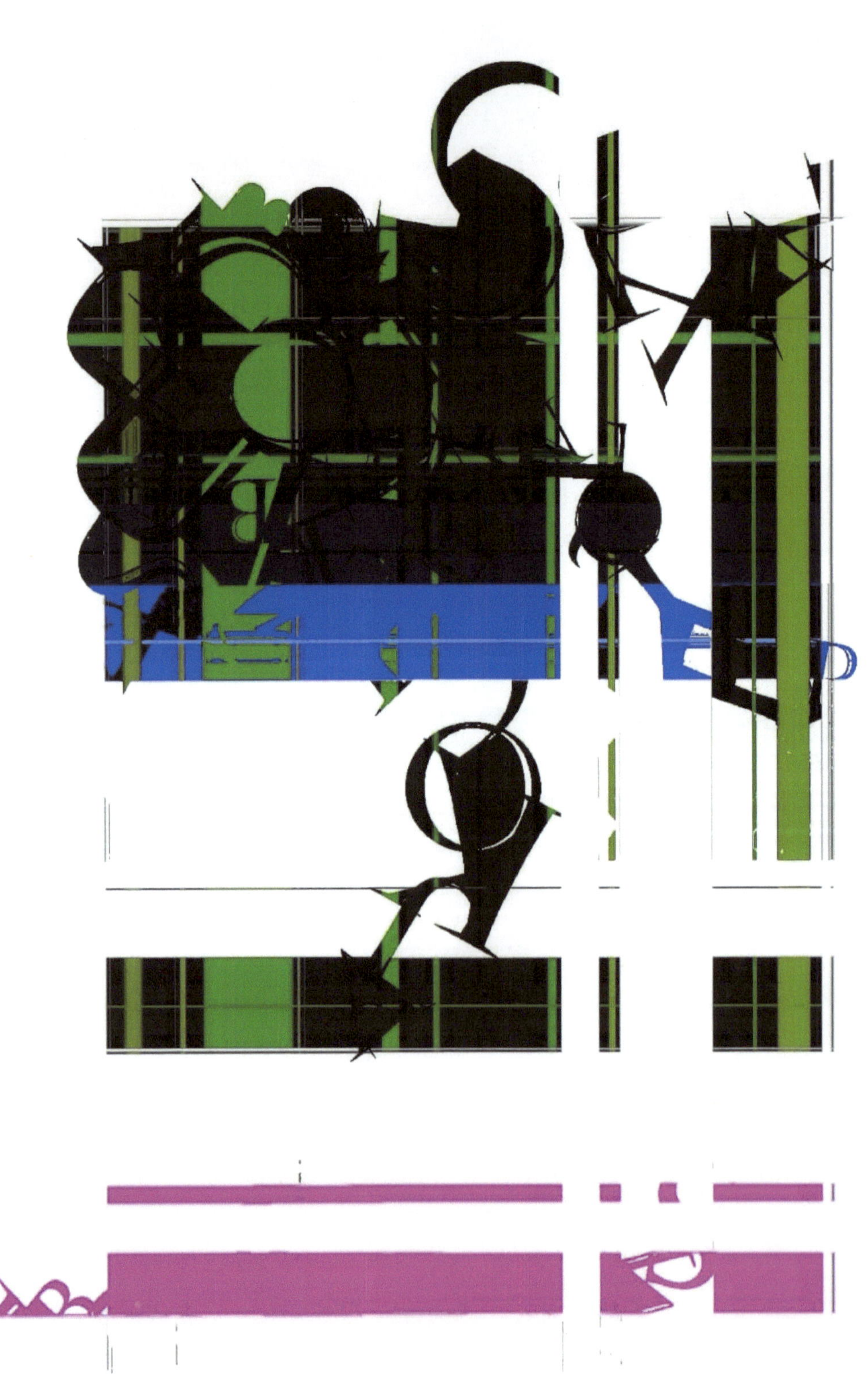

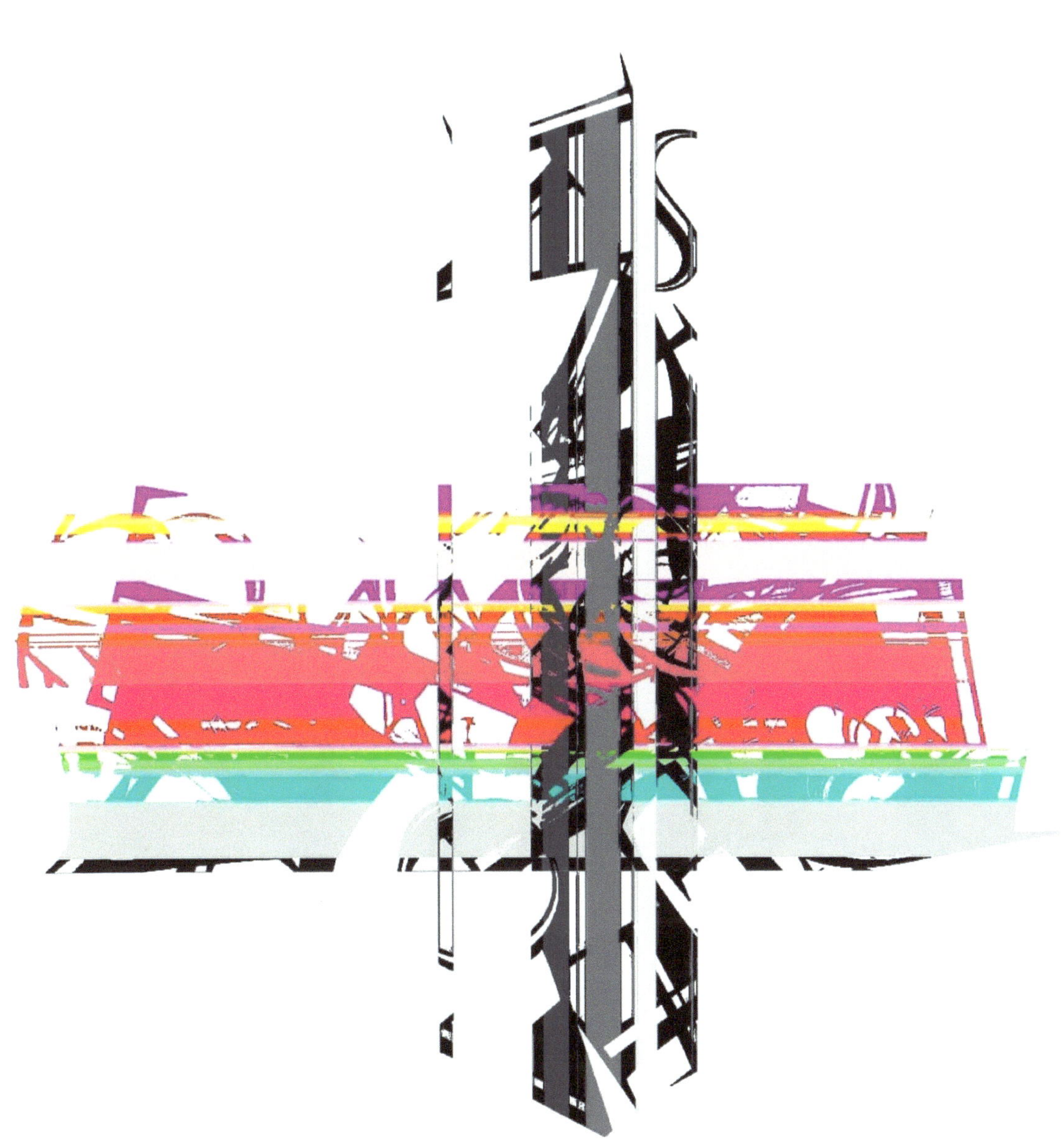

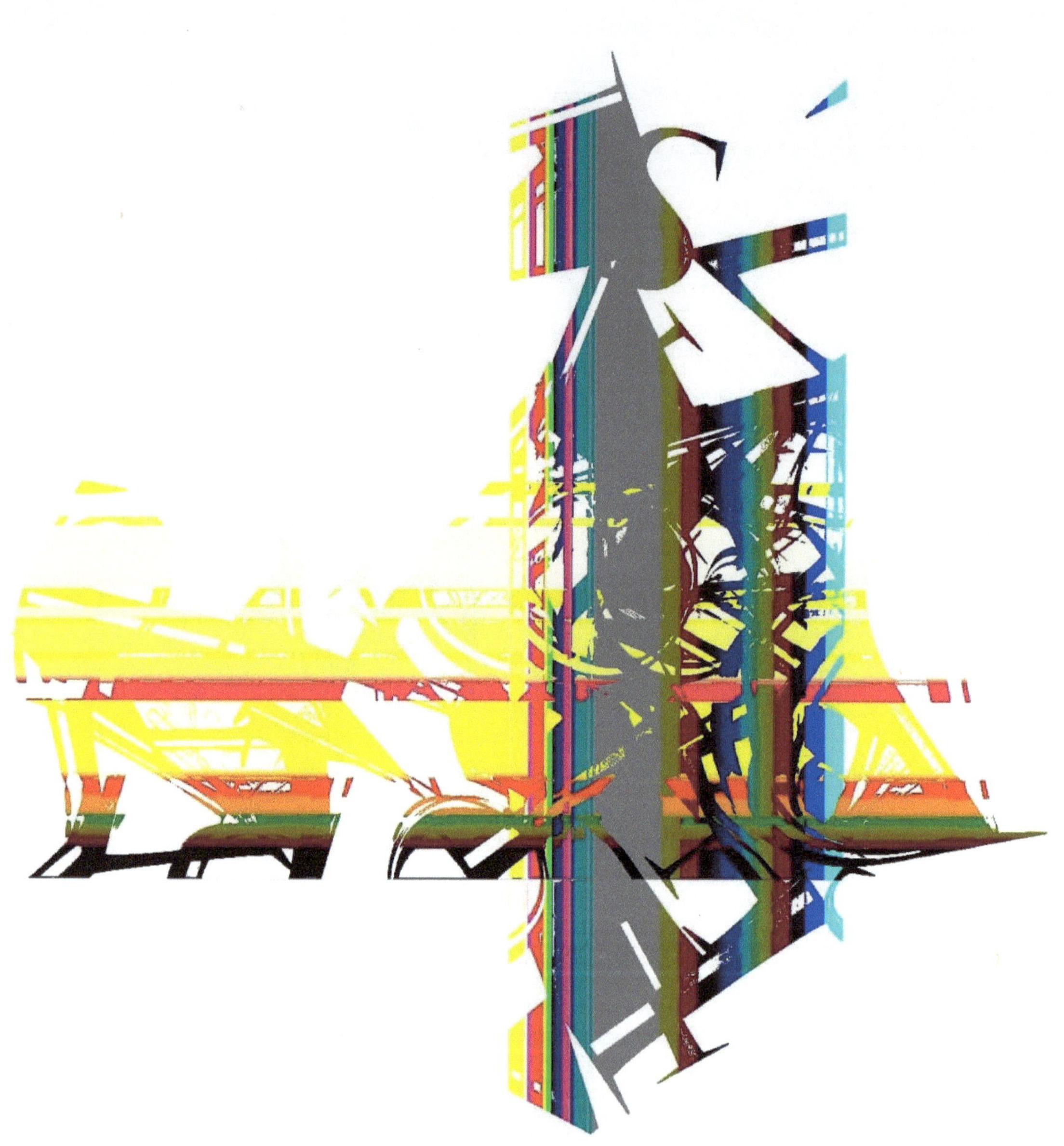

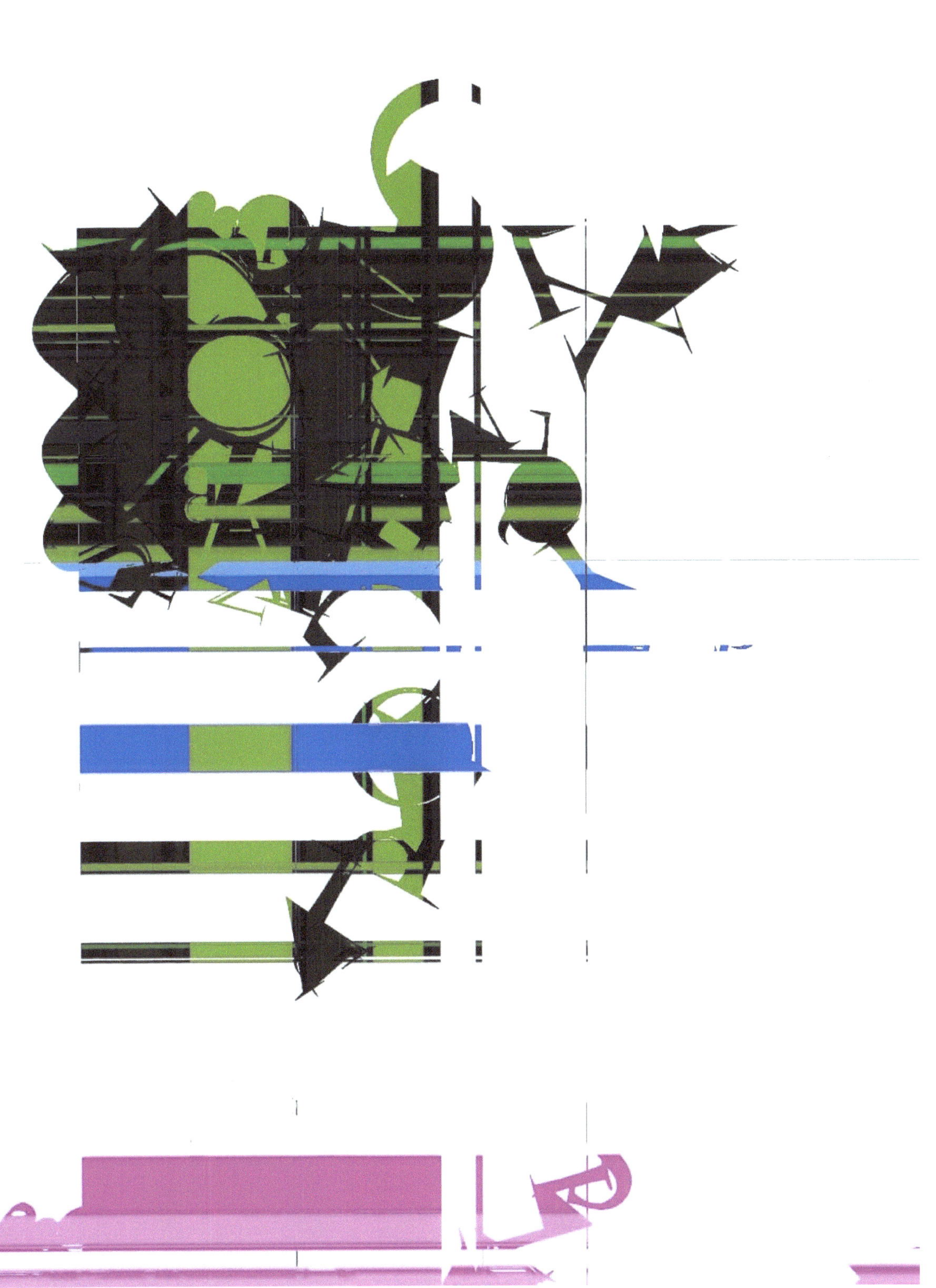

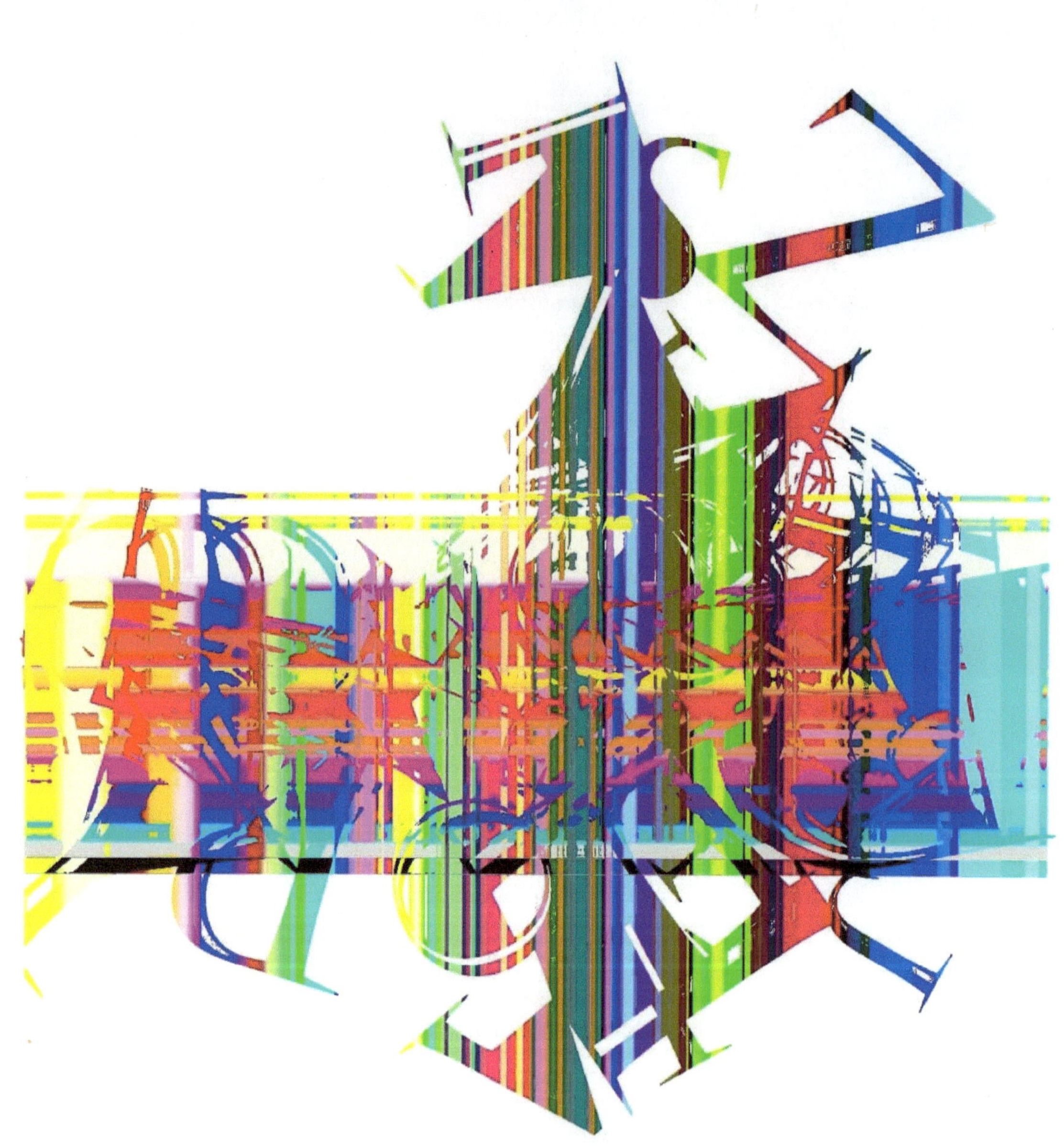

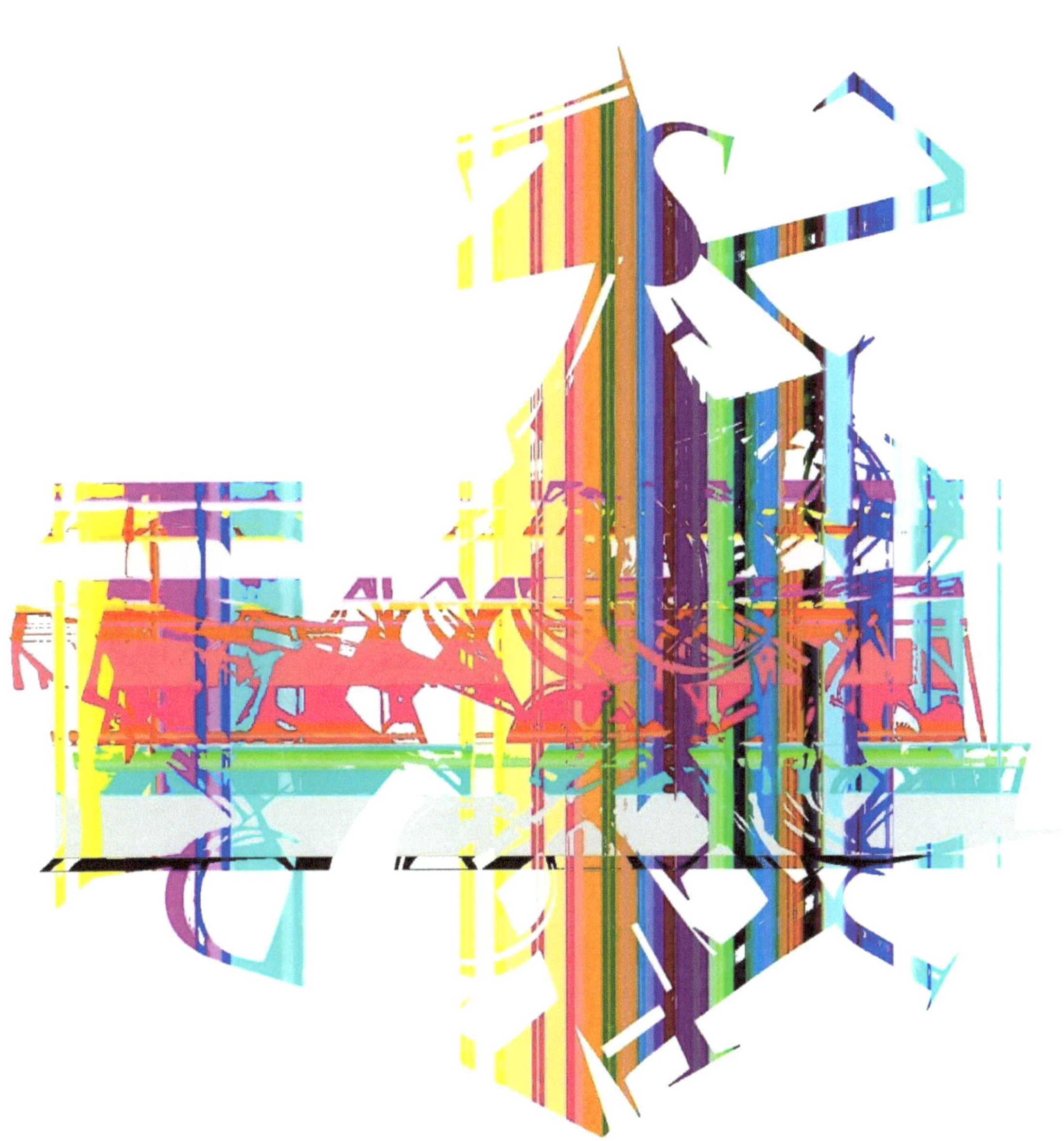

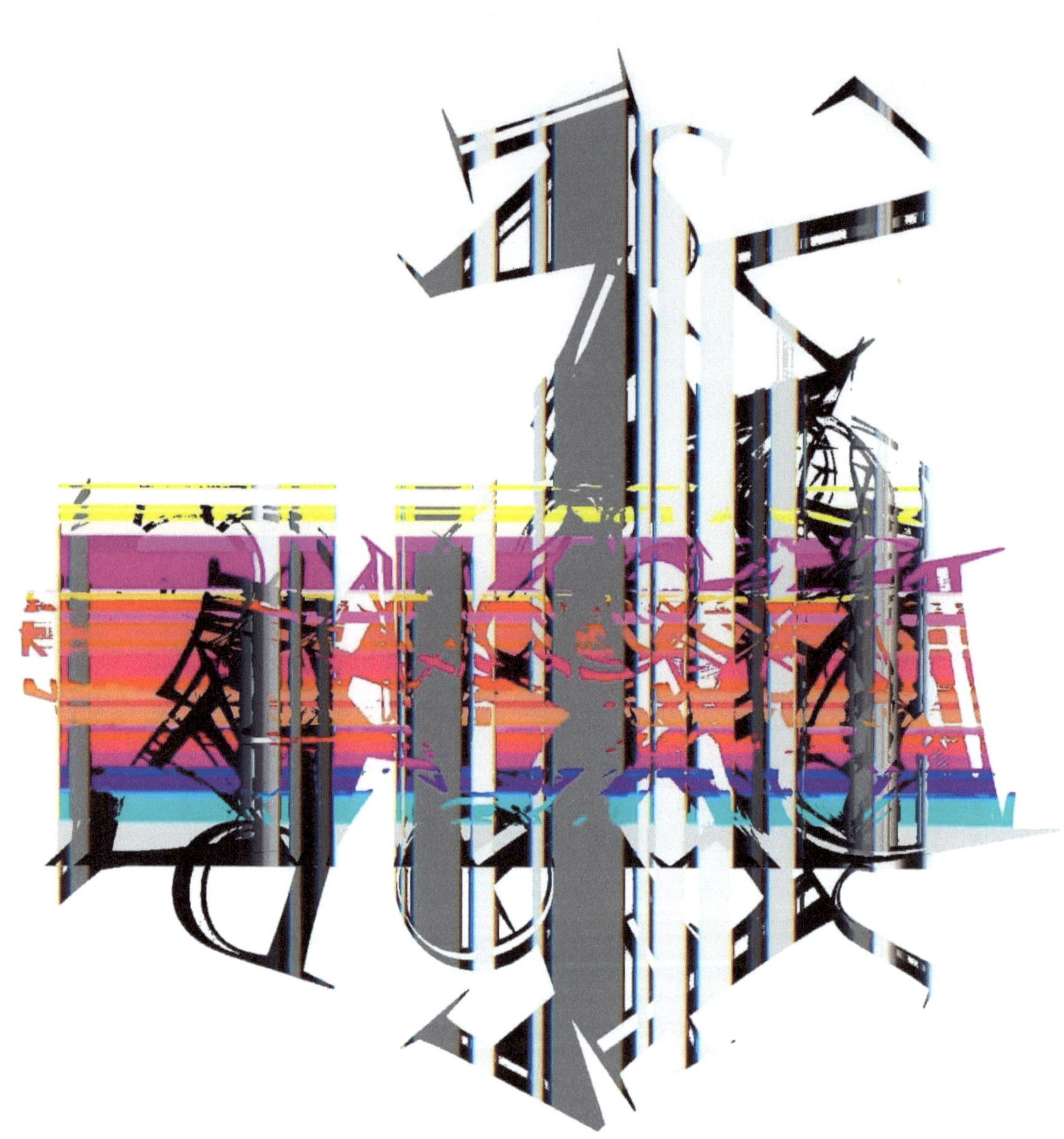

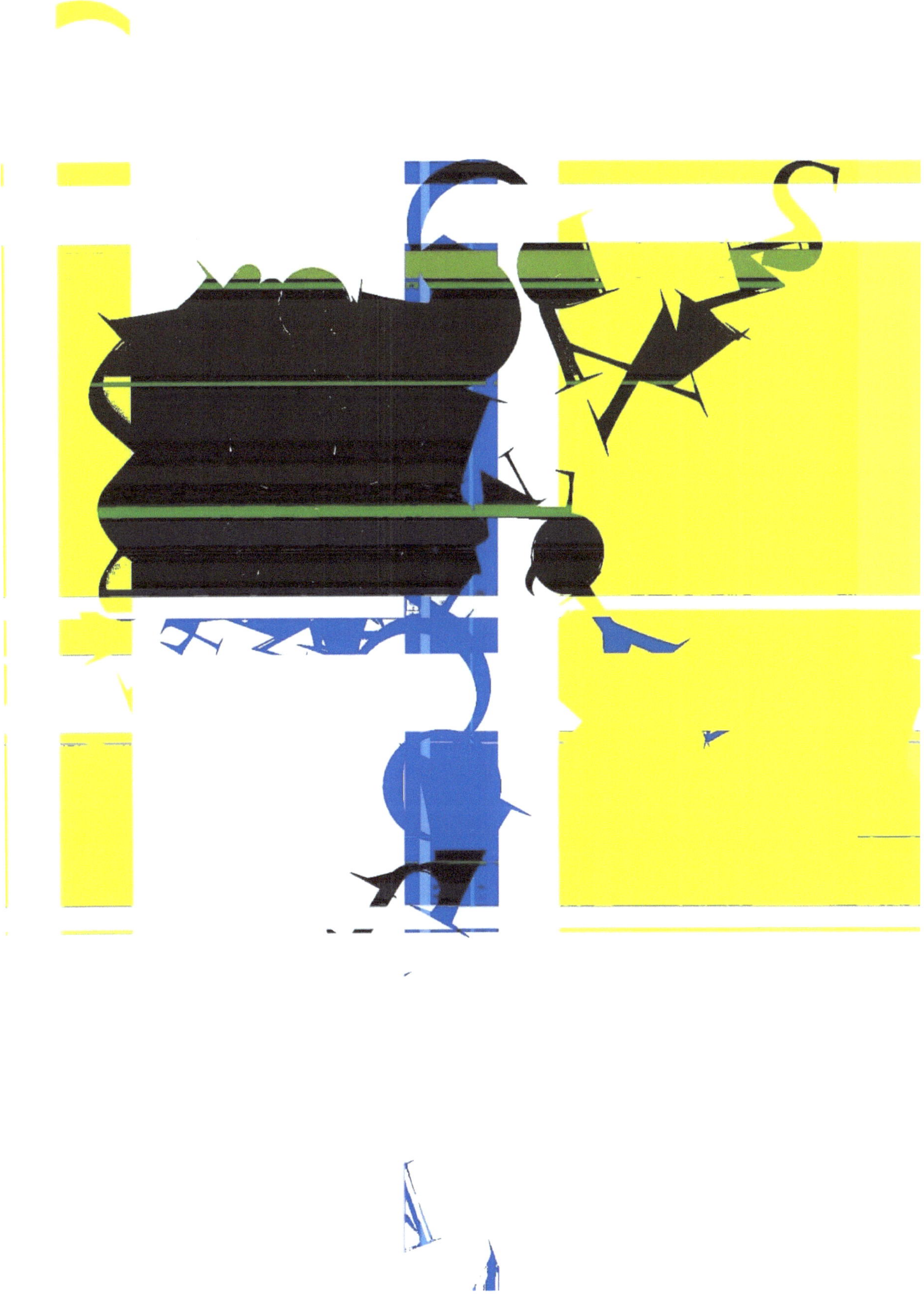

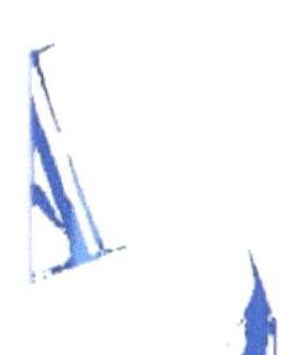

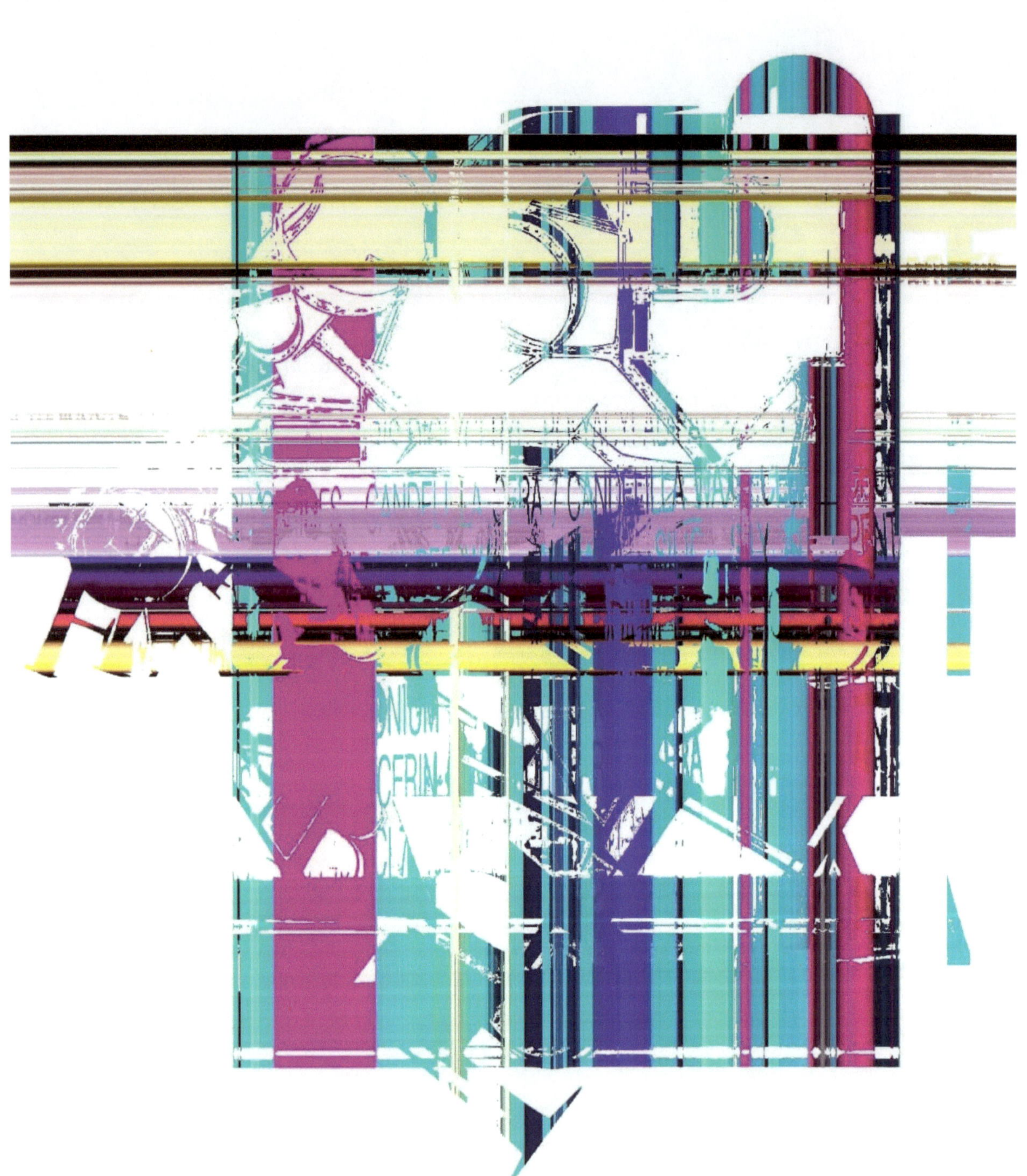
CANDELILLA
CANDELILLA WAX
NIGM
CFRIN

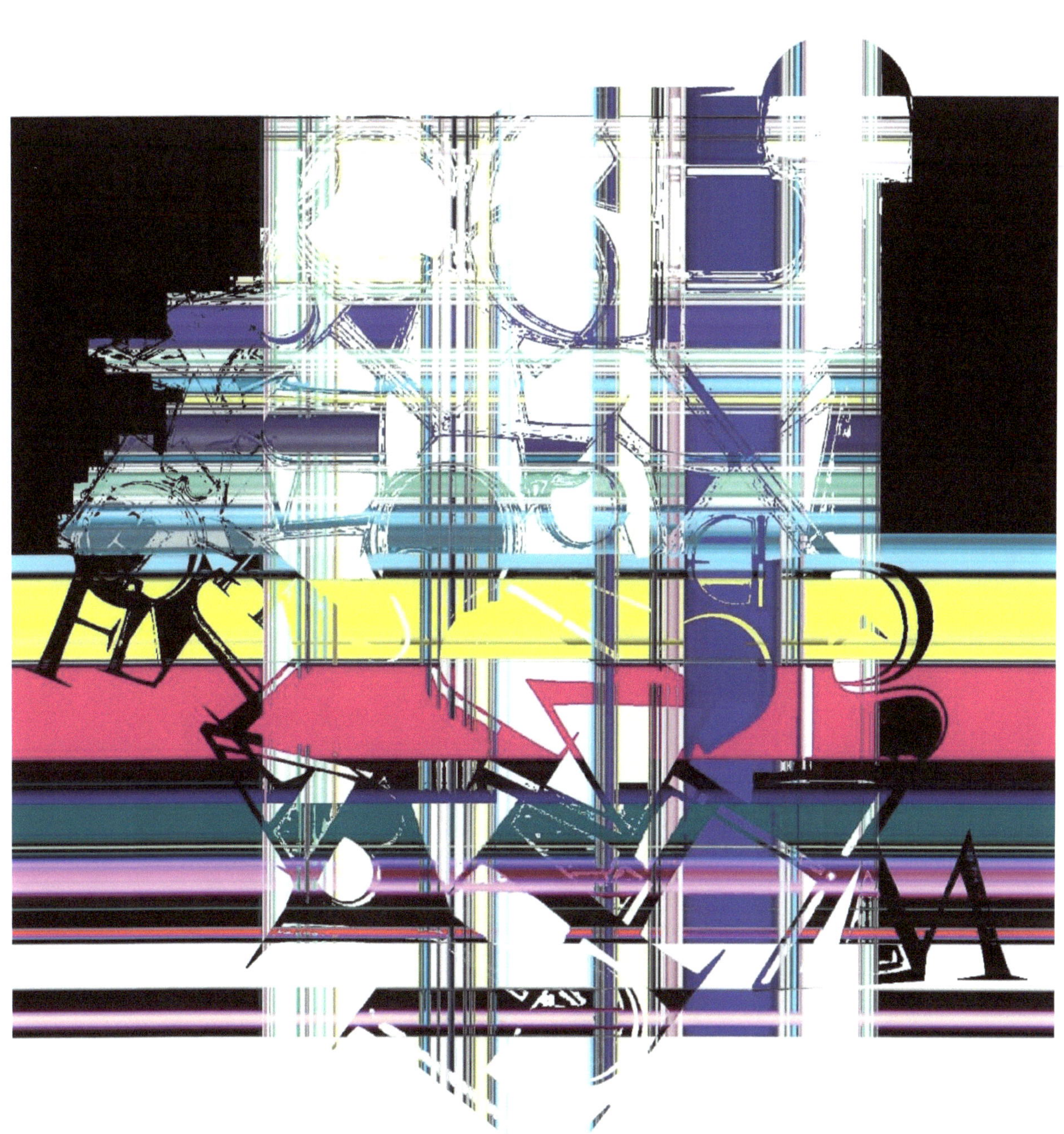

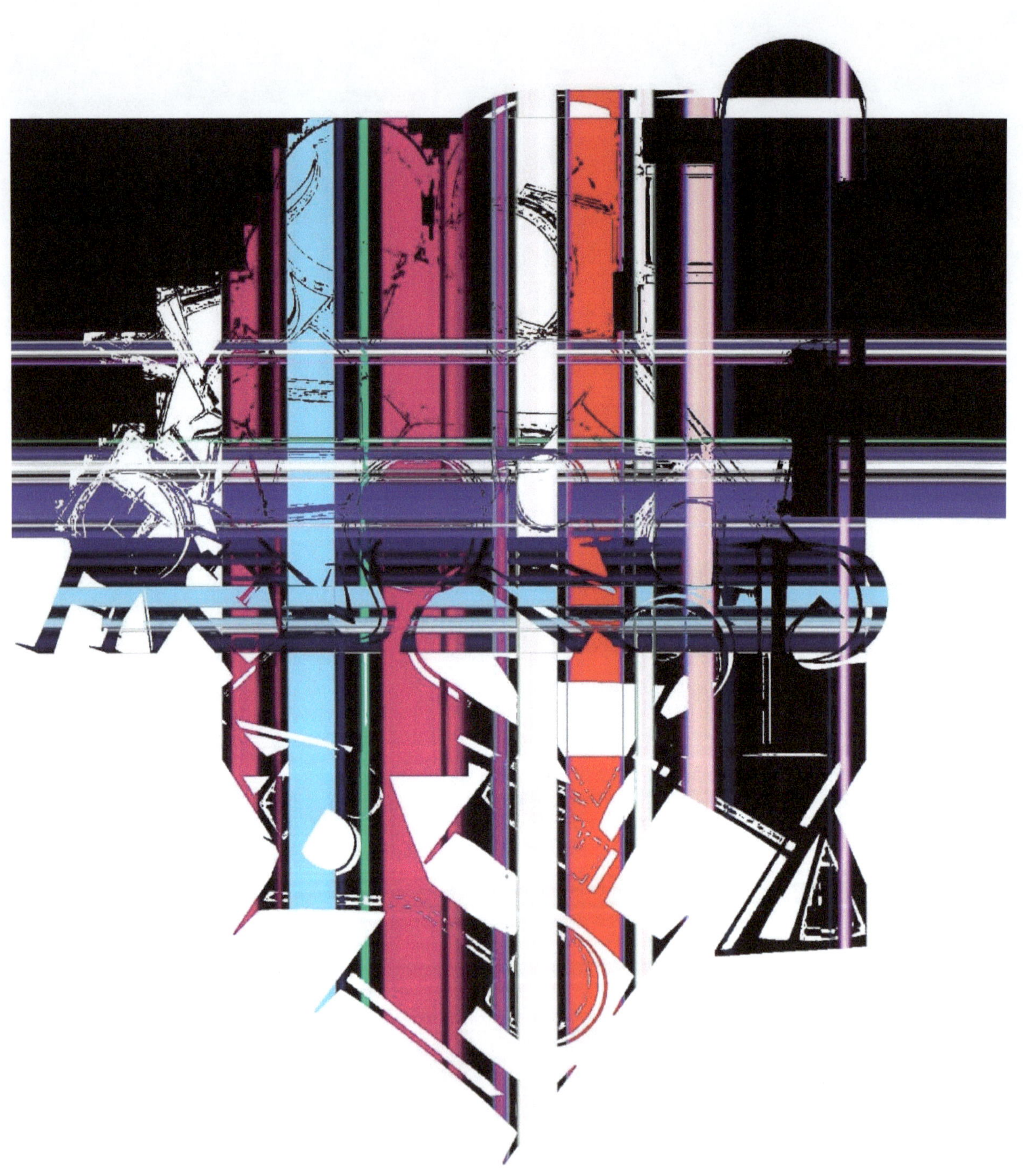

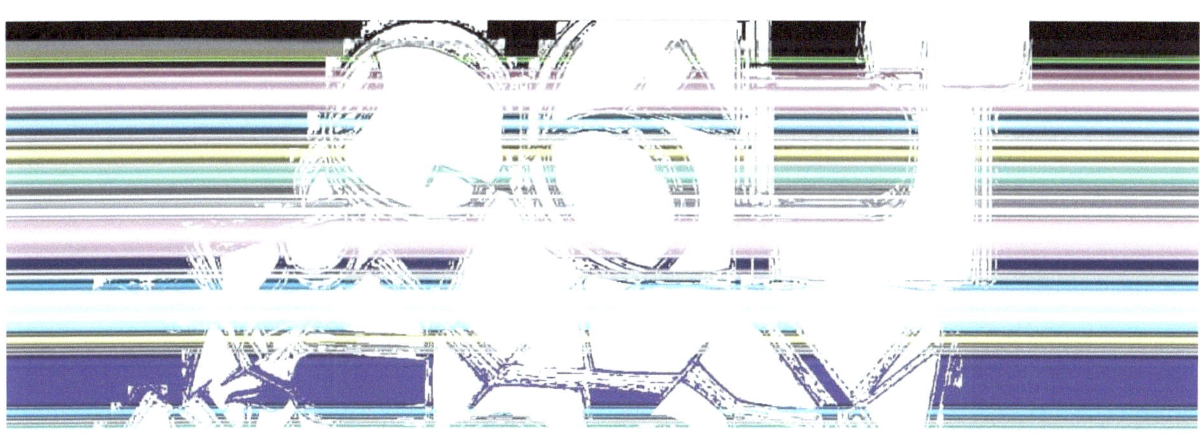
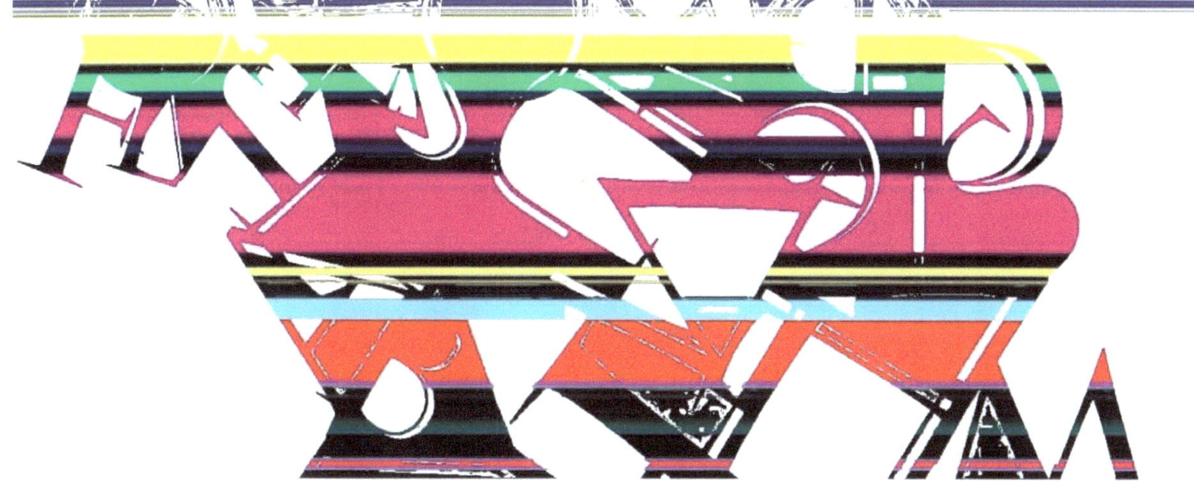

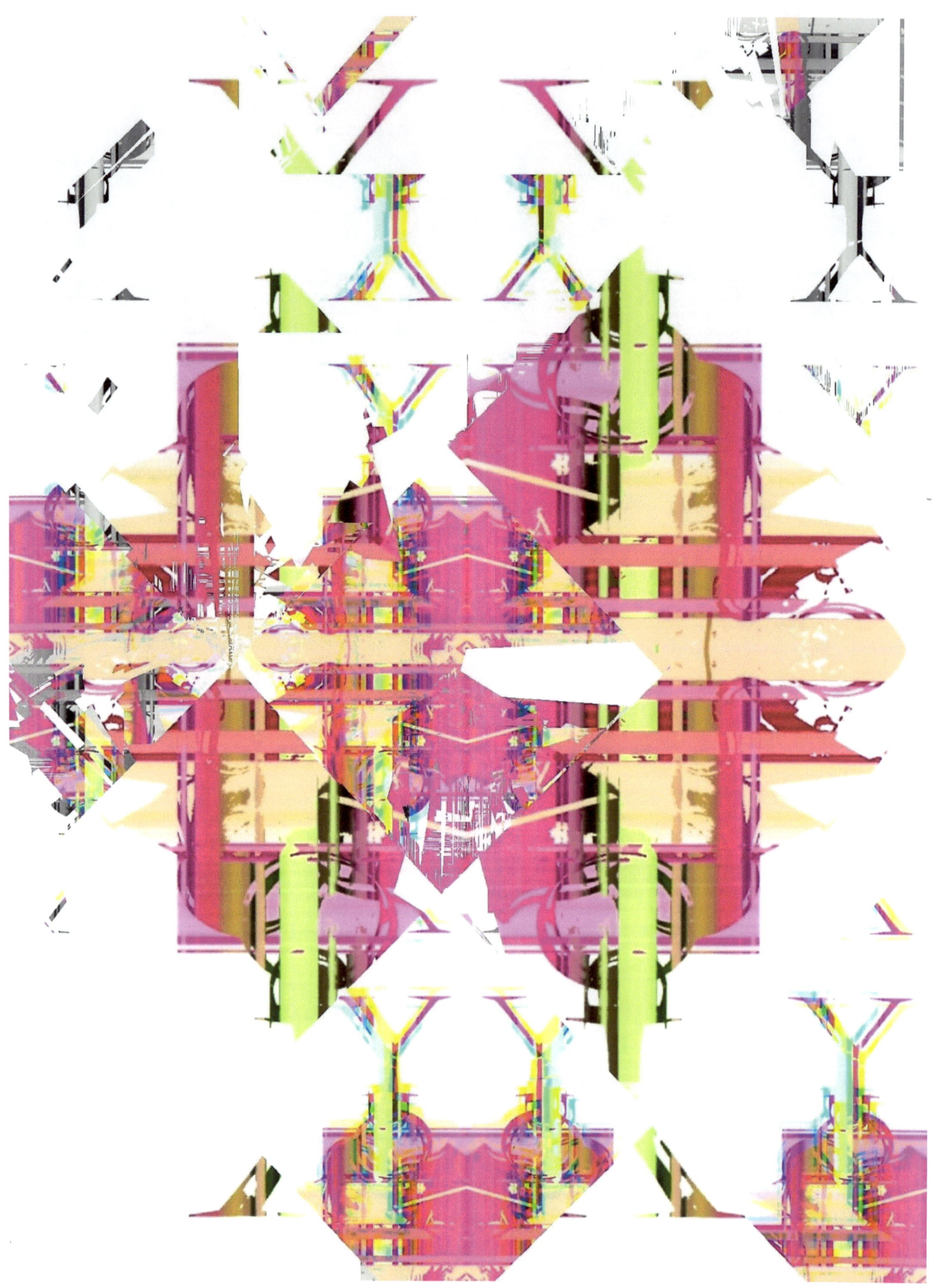

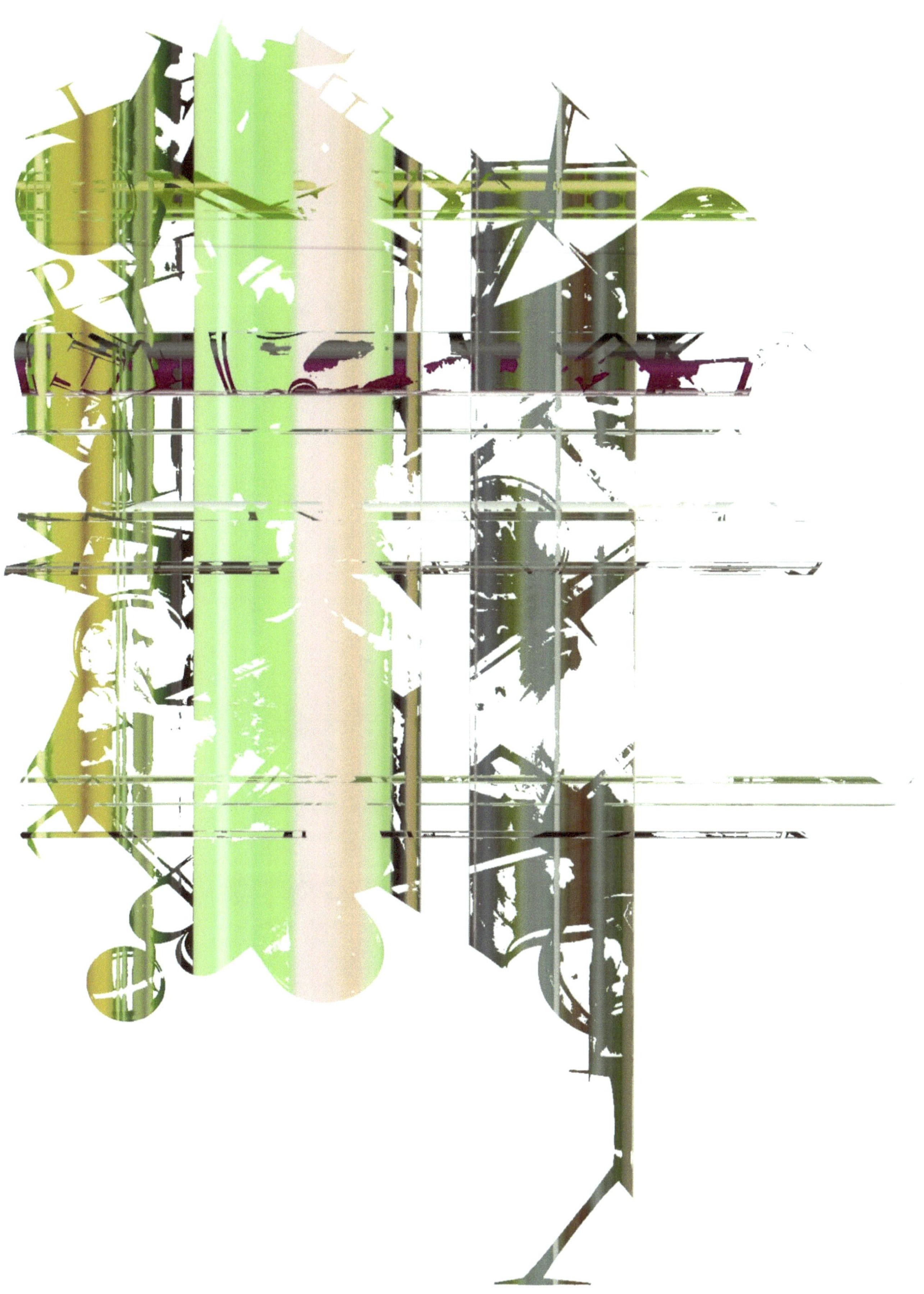

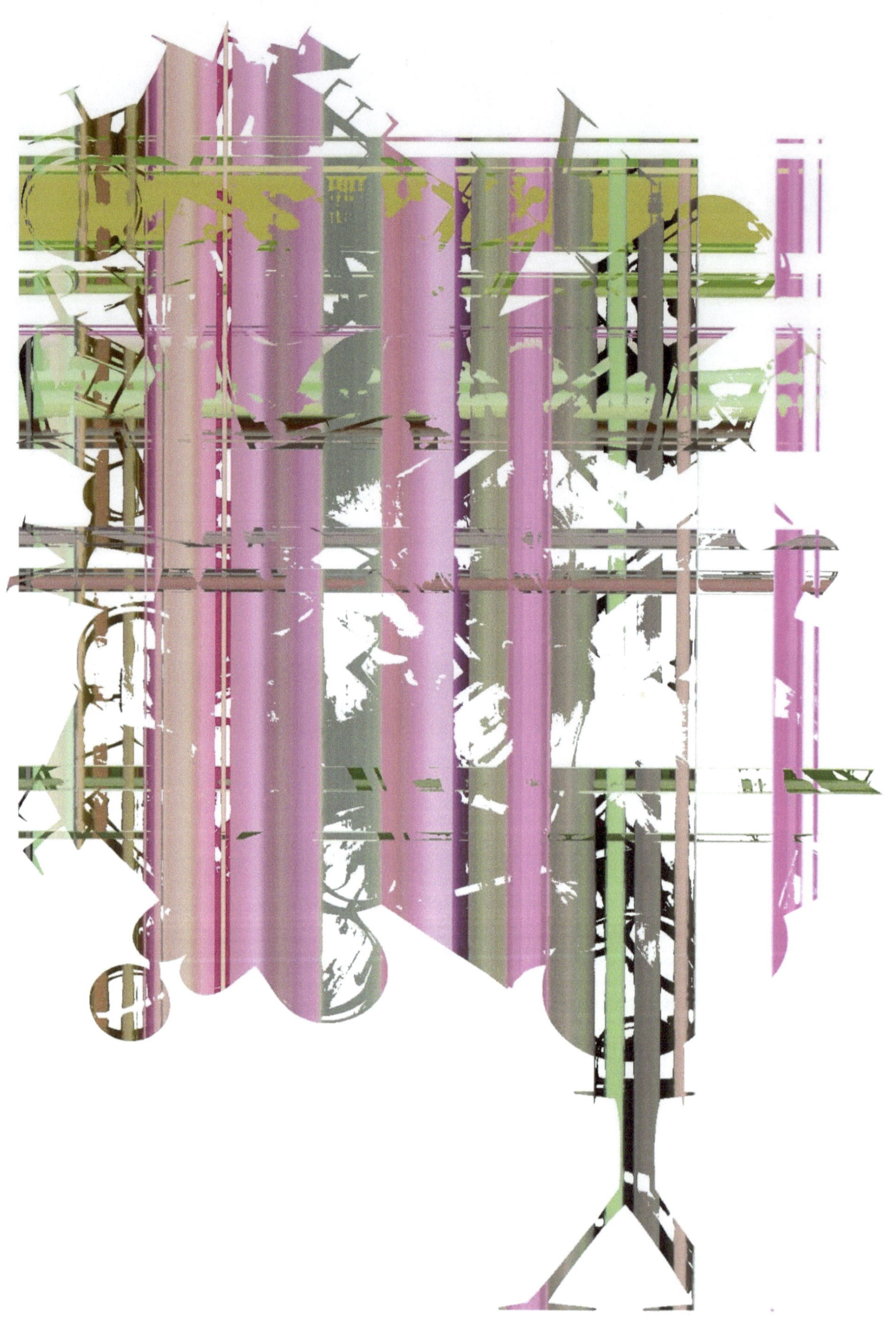

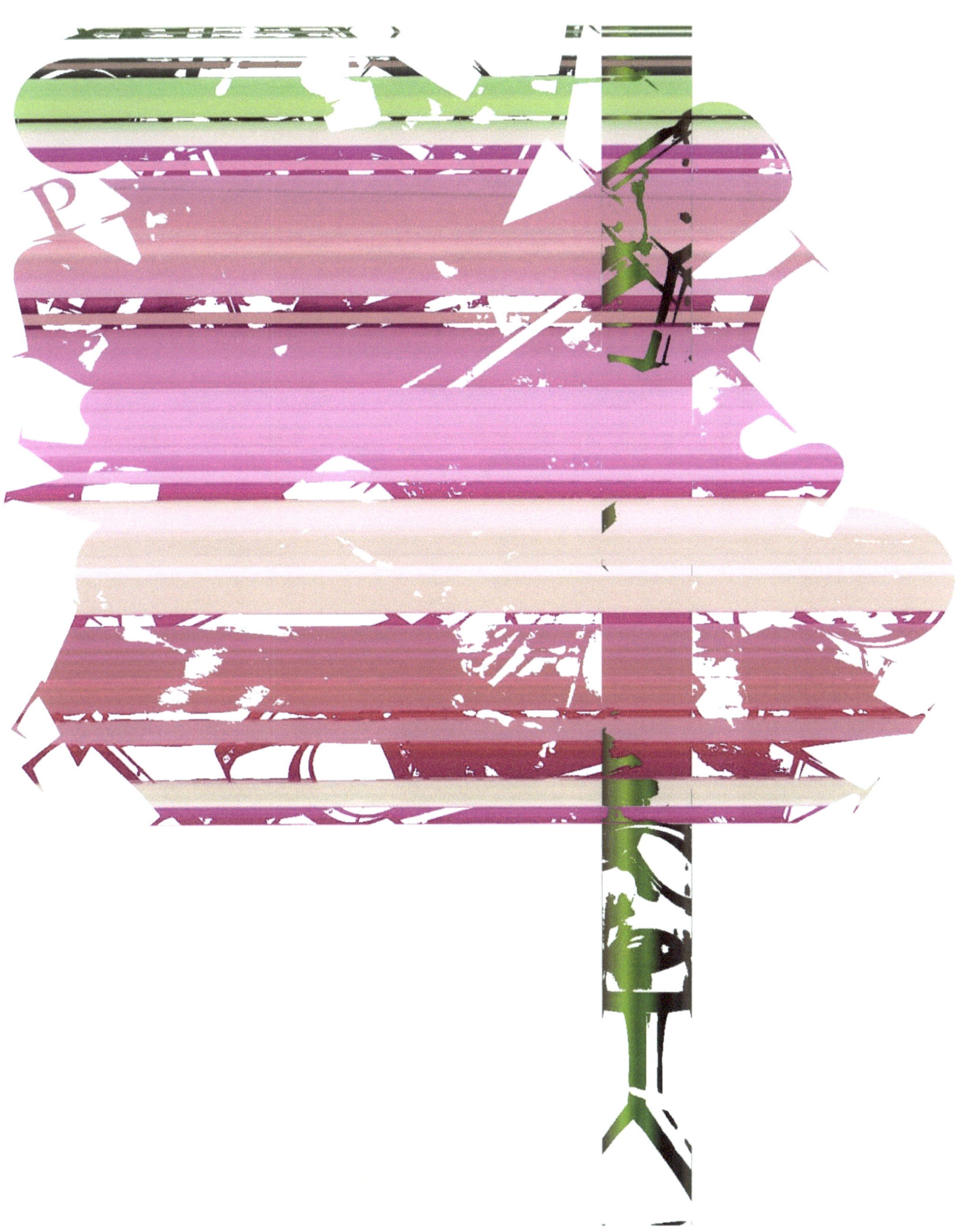

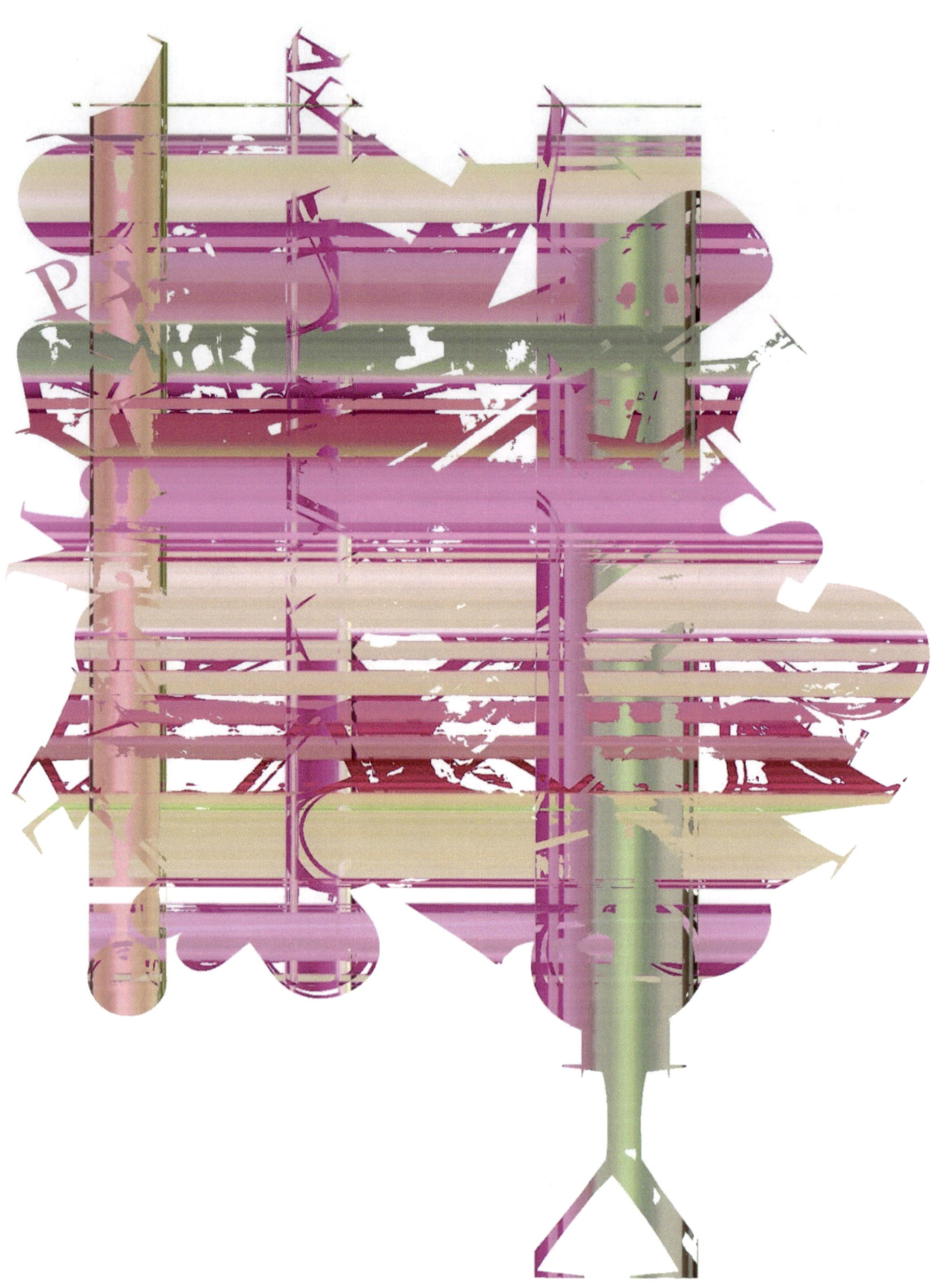

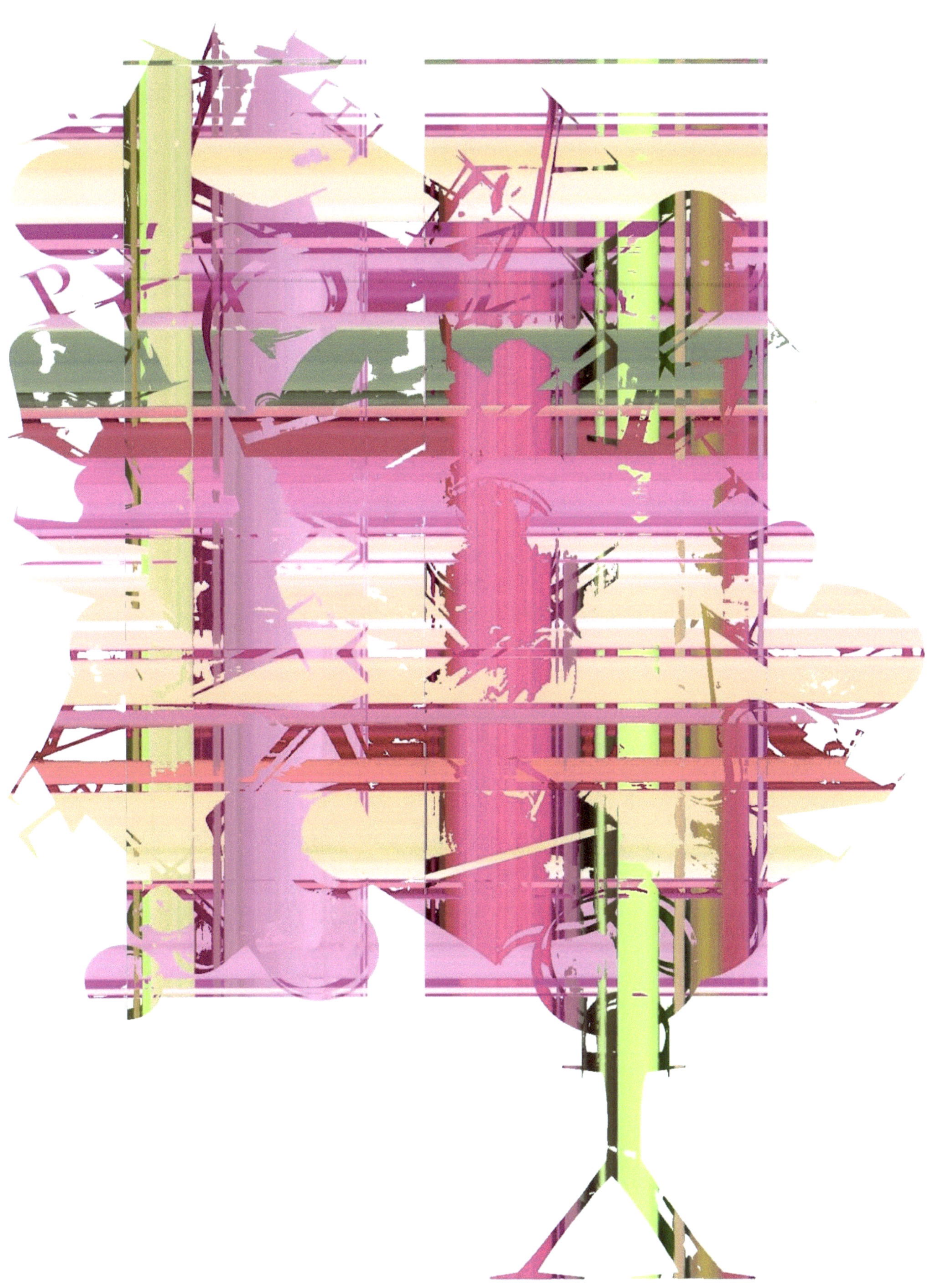

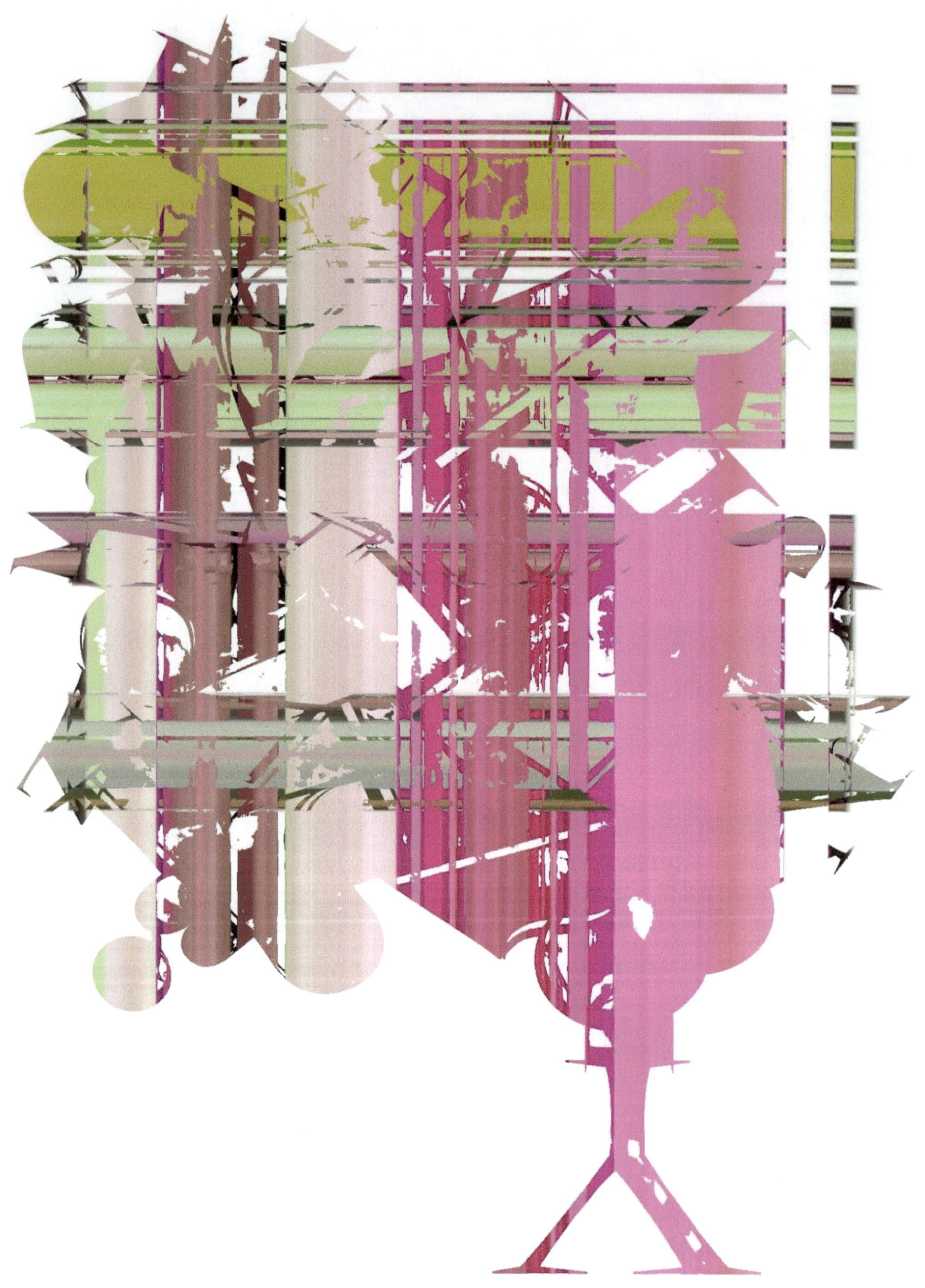

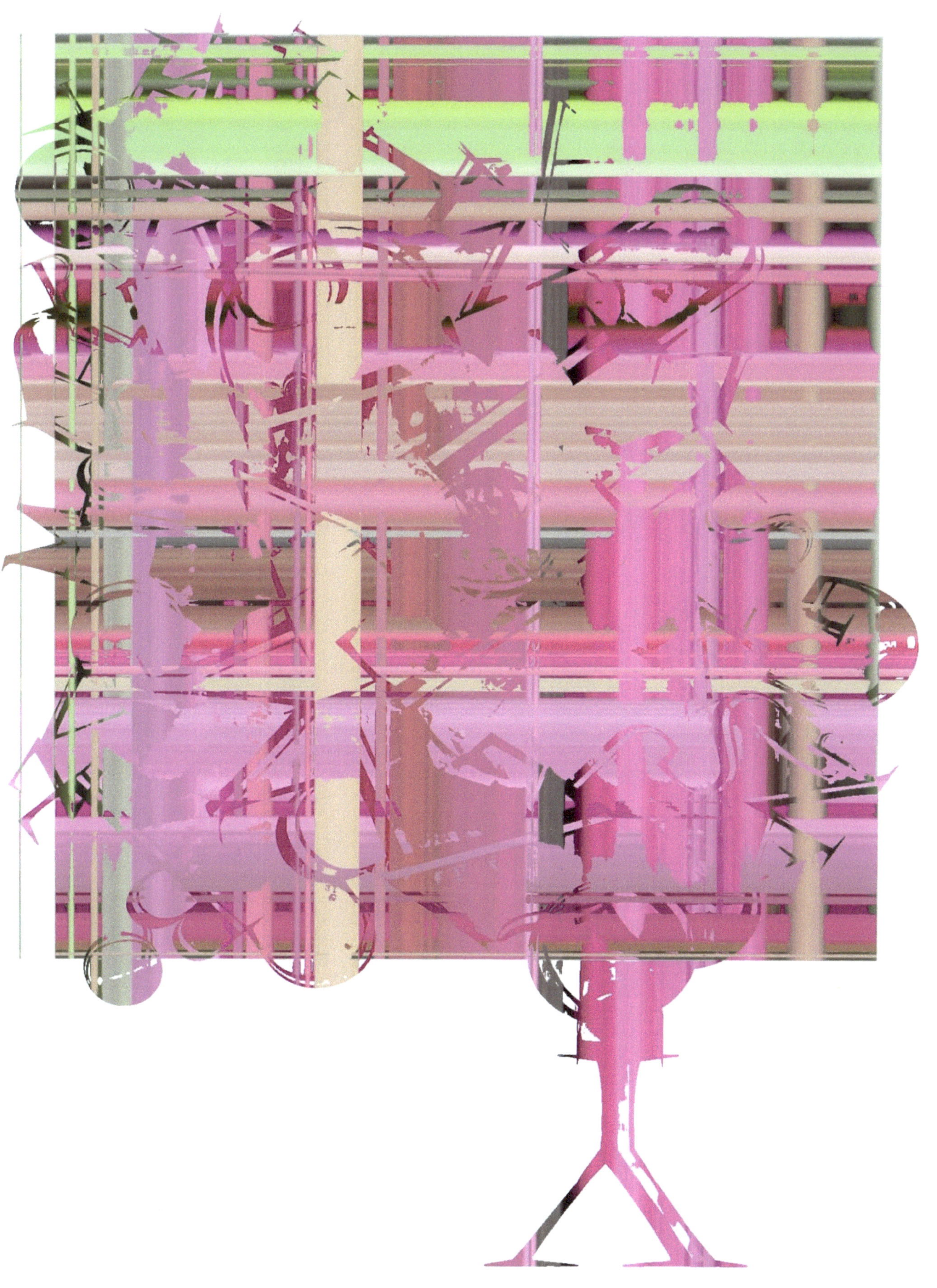

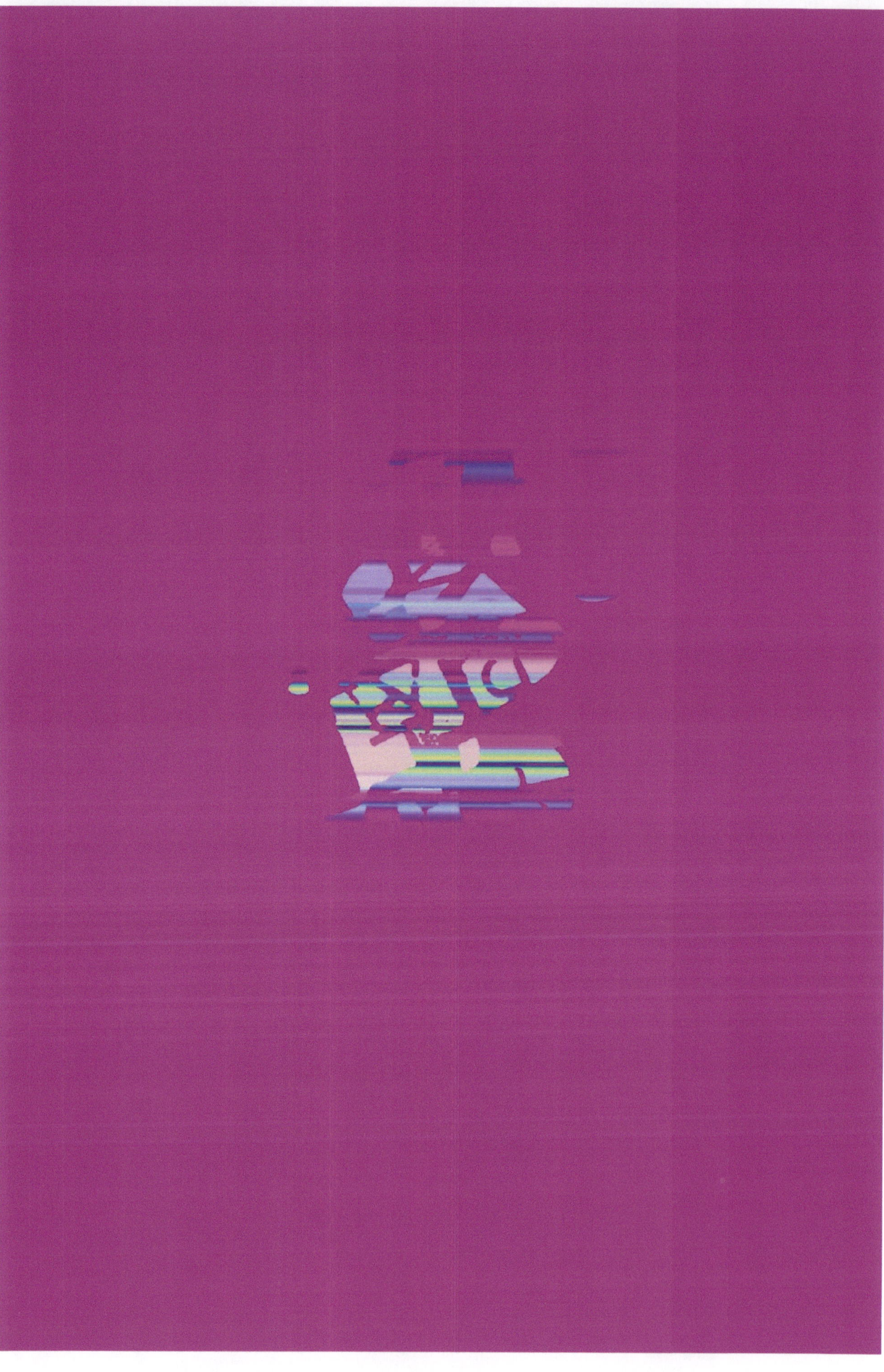

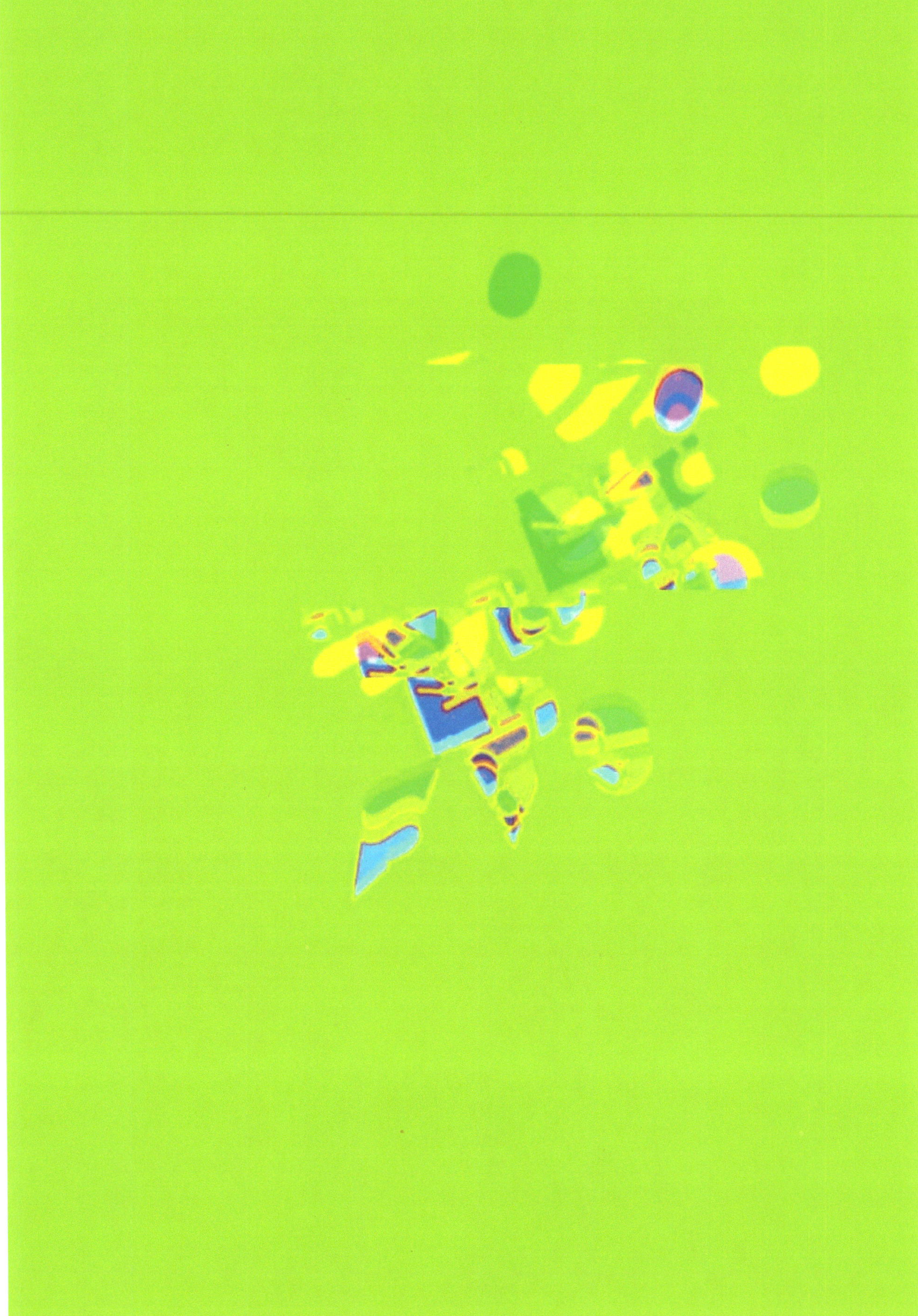

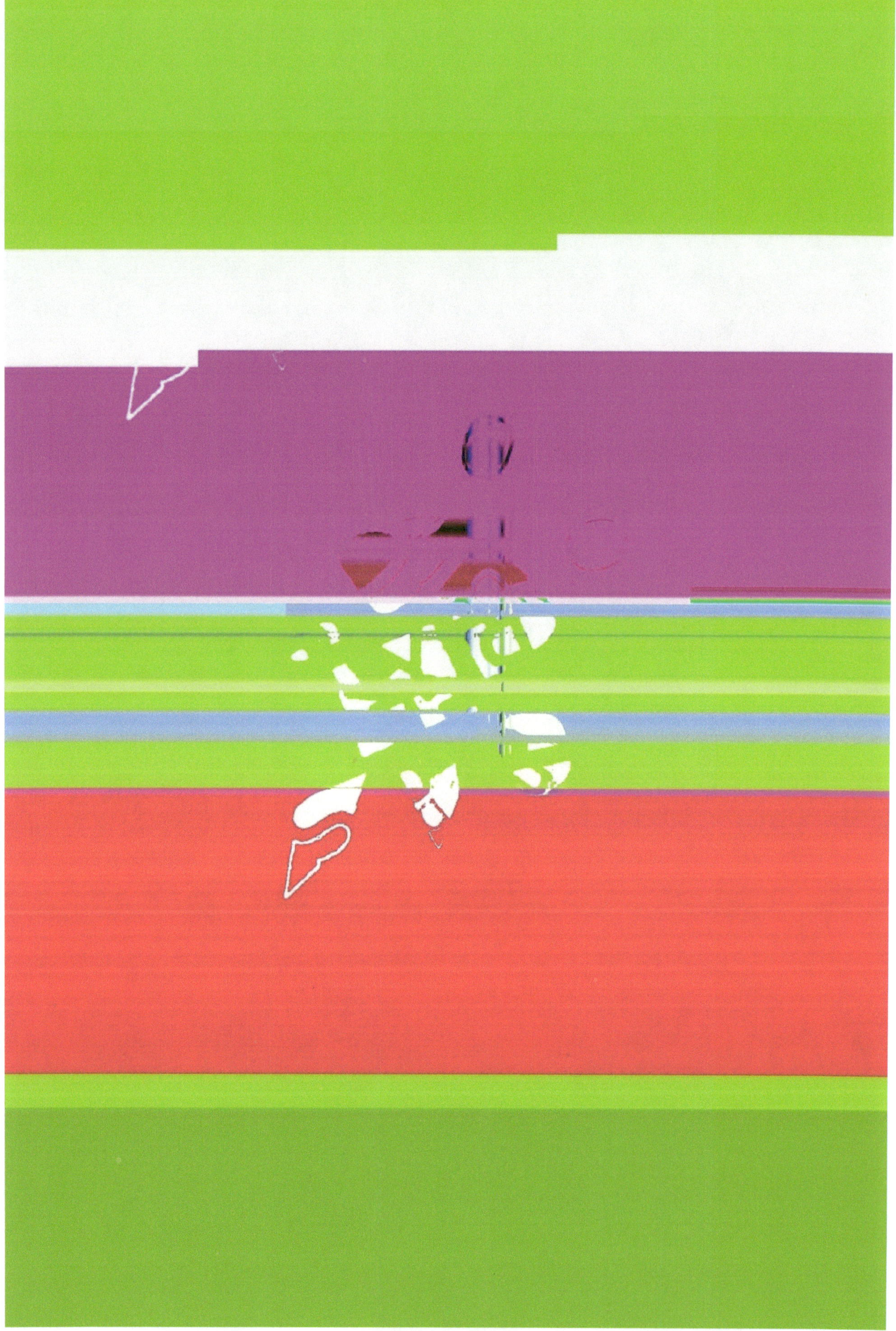

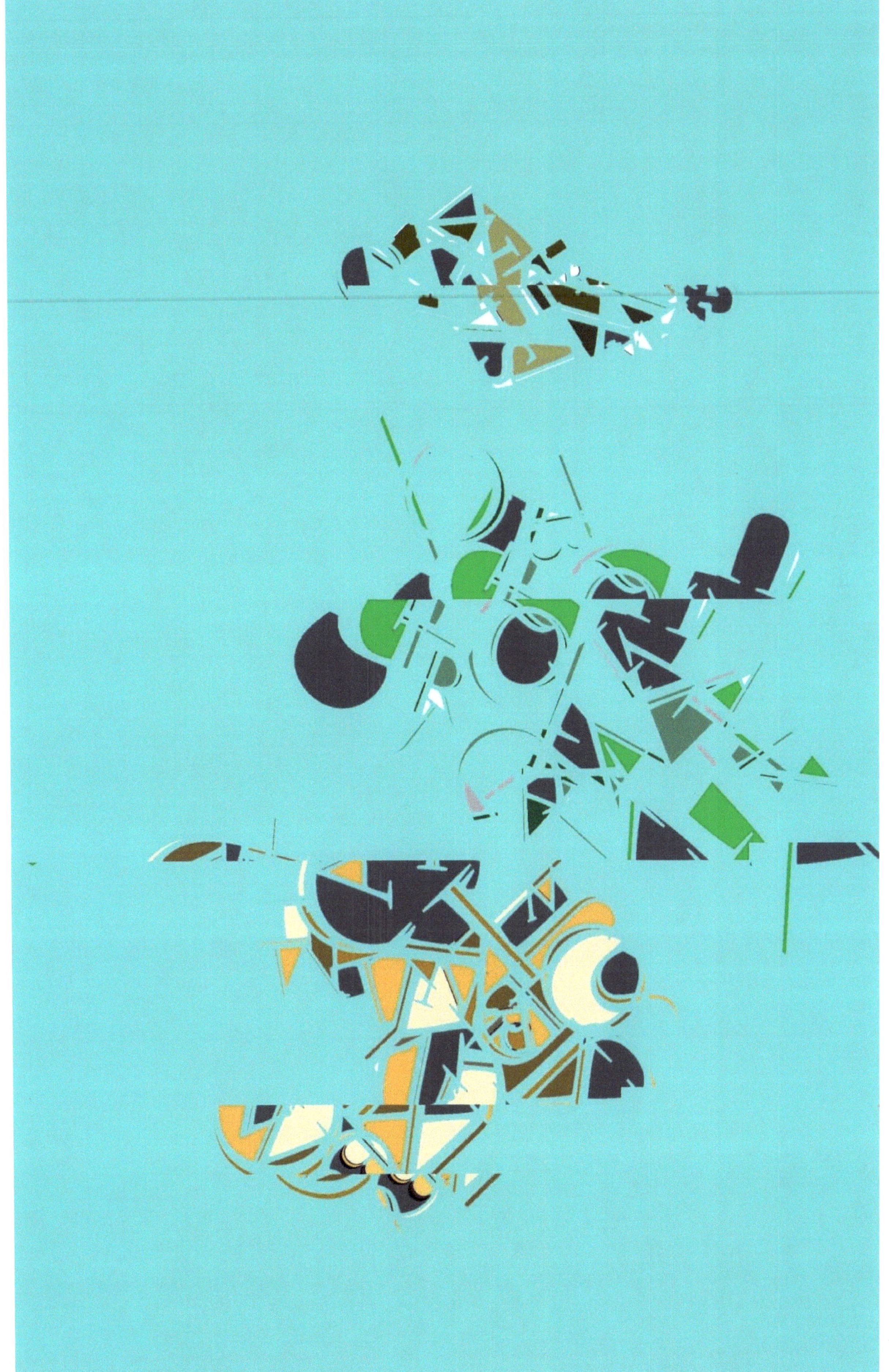

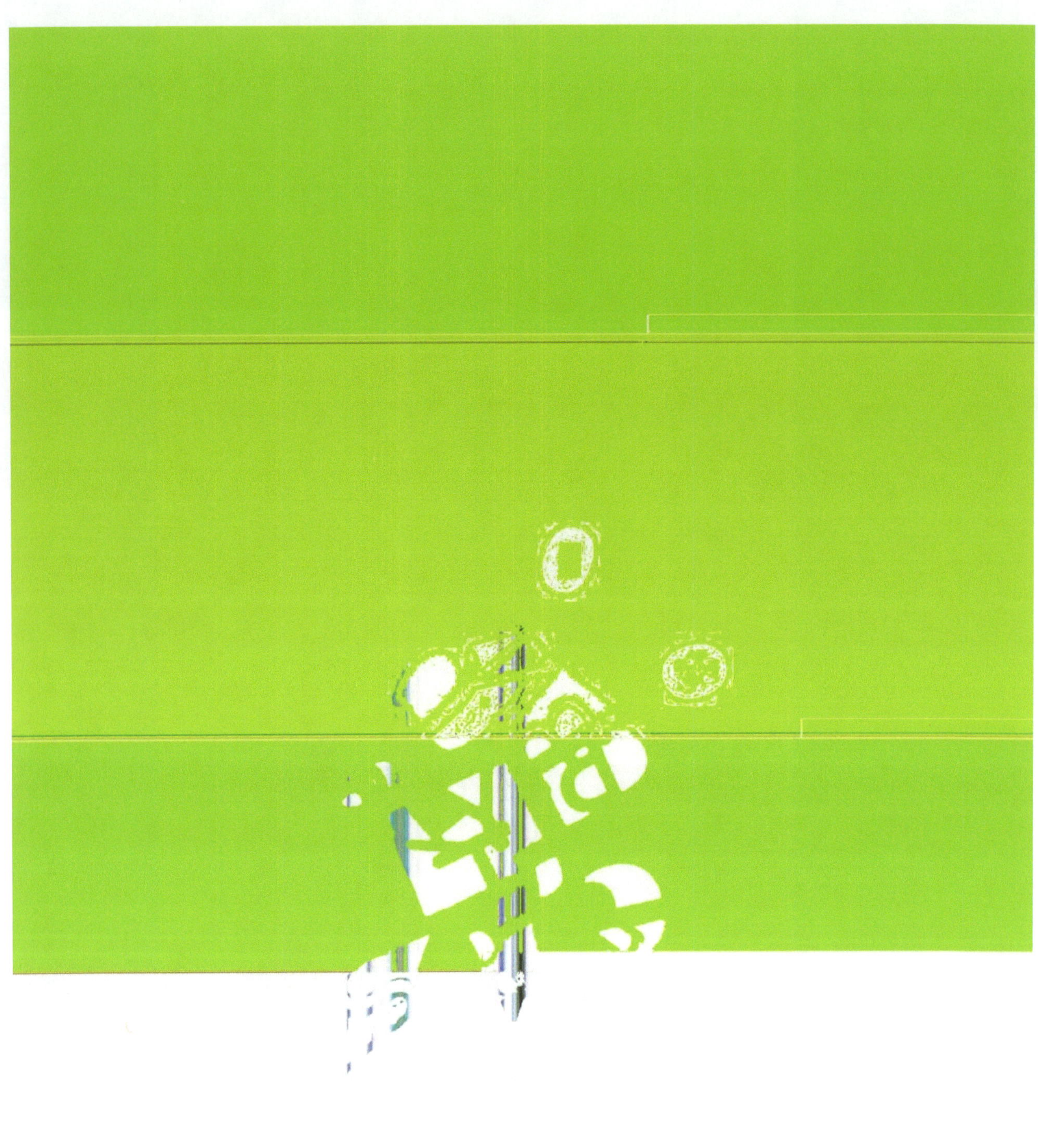

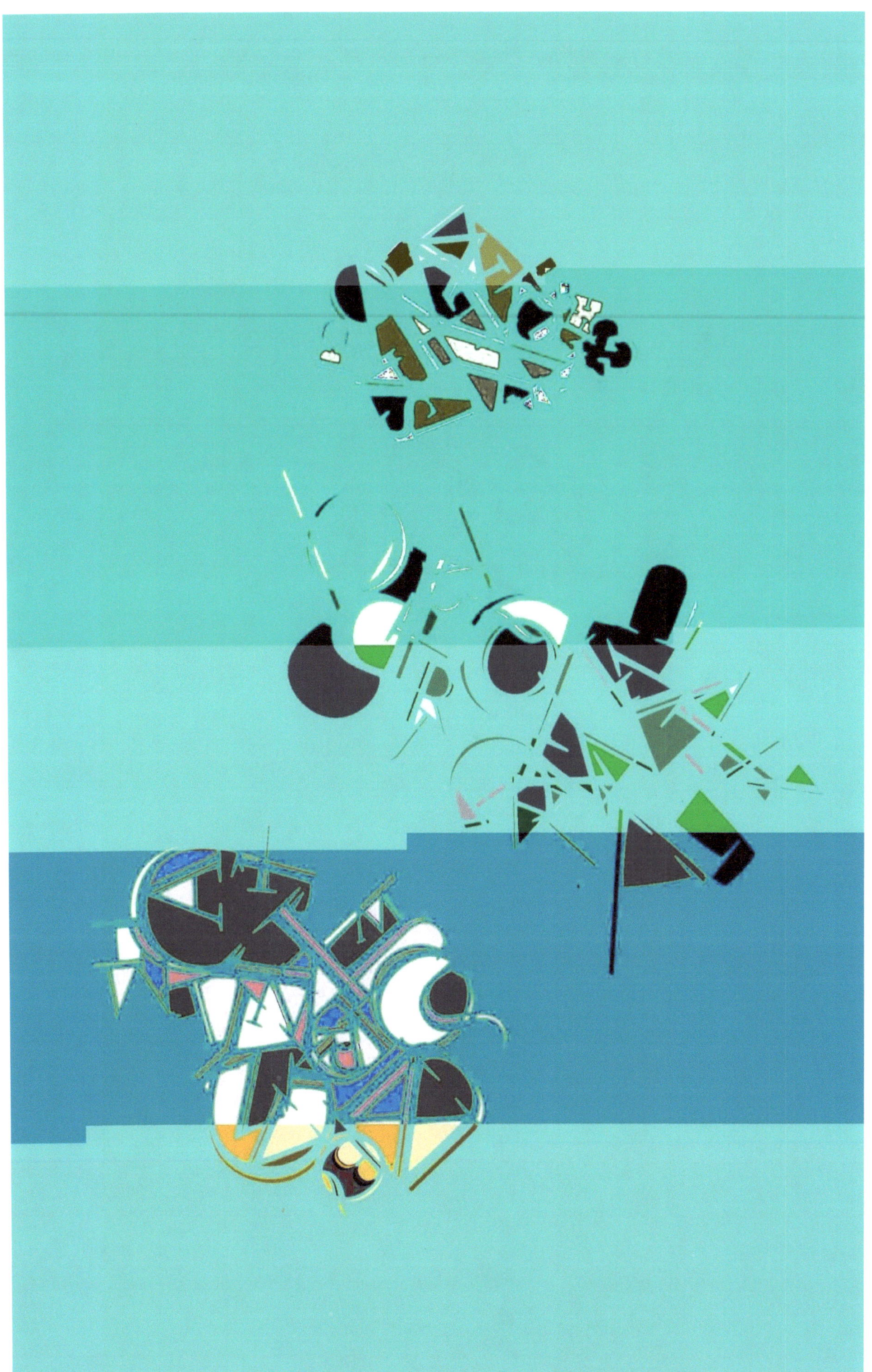

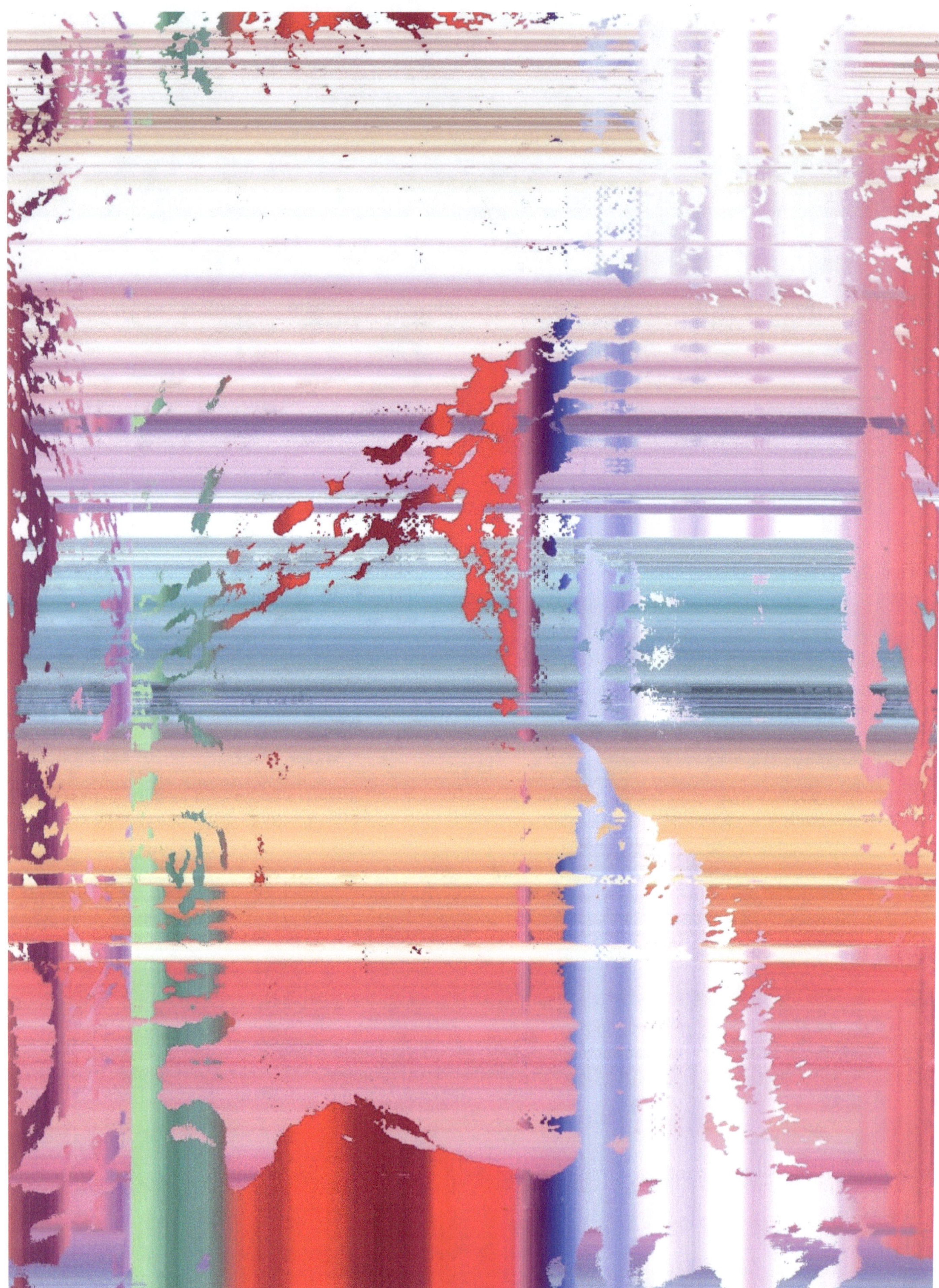

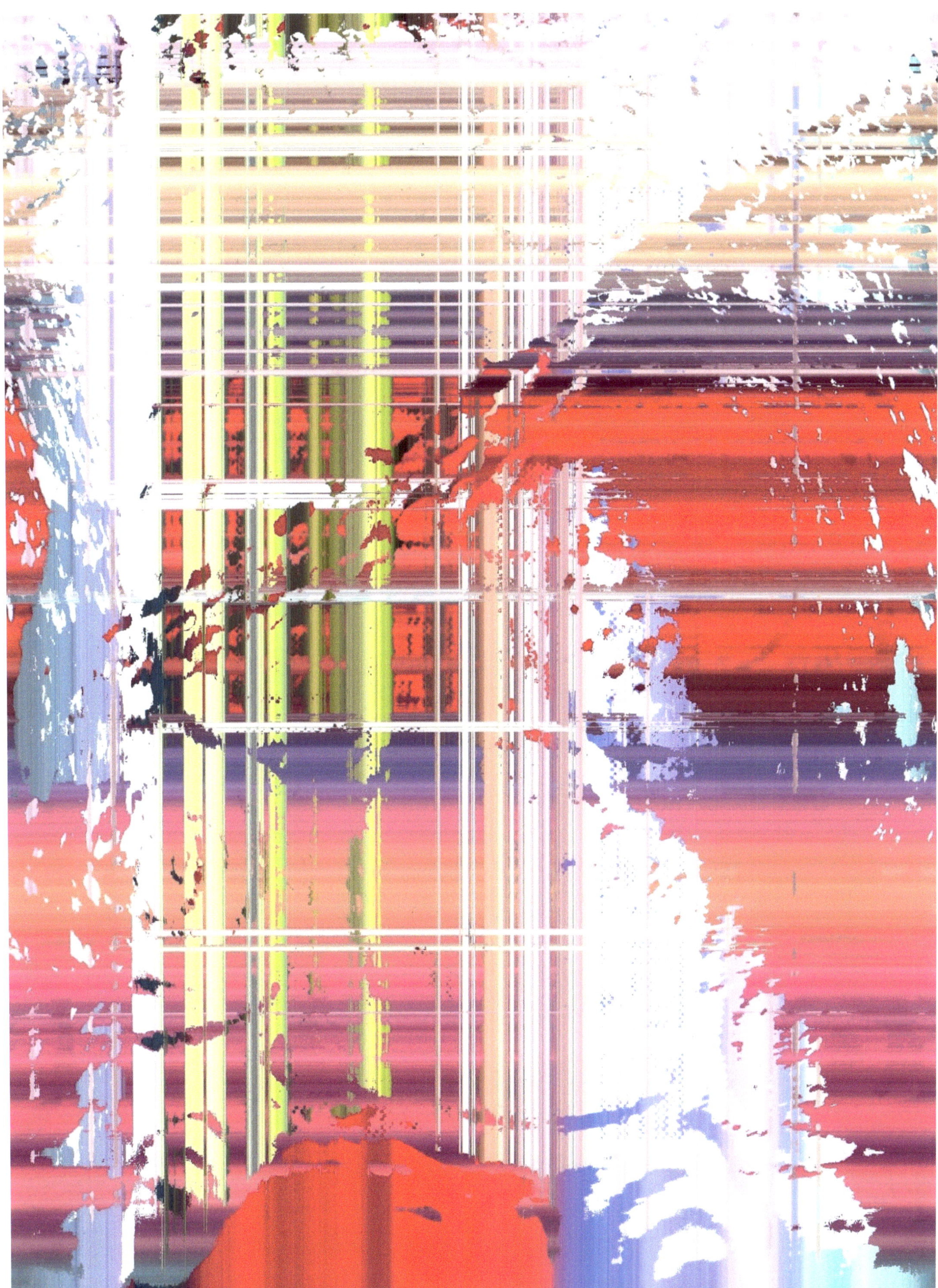

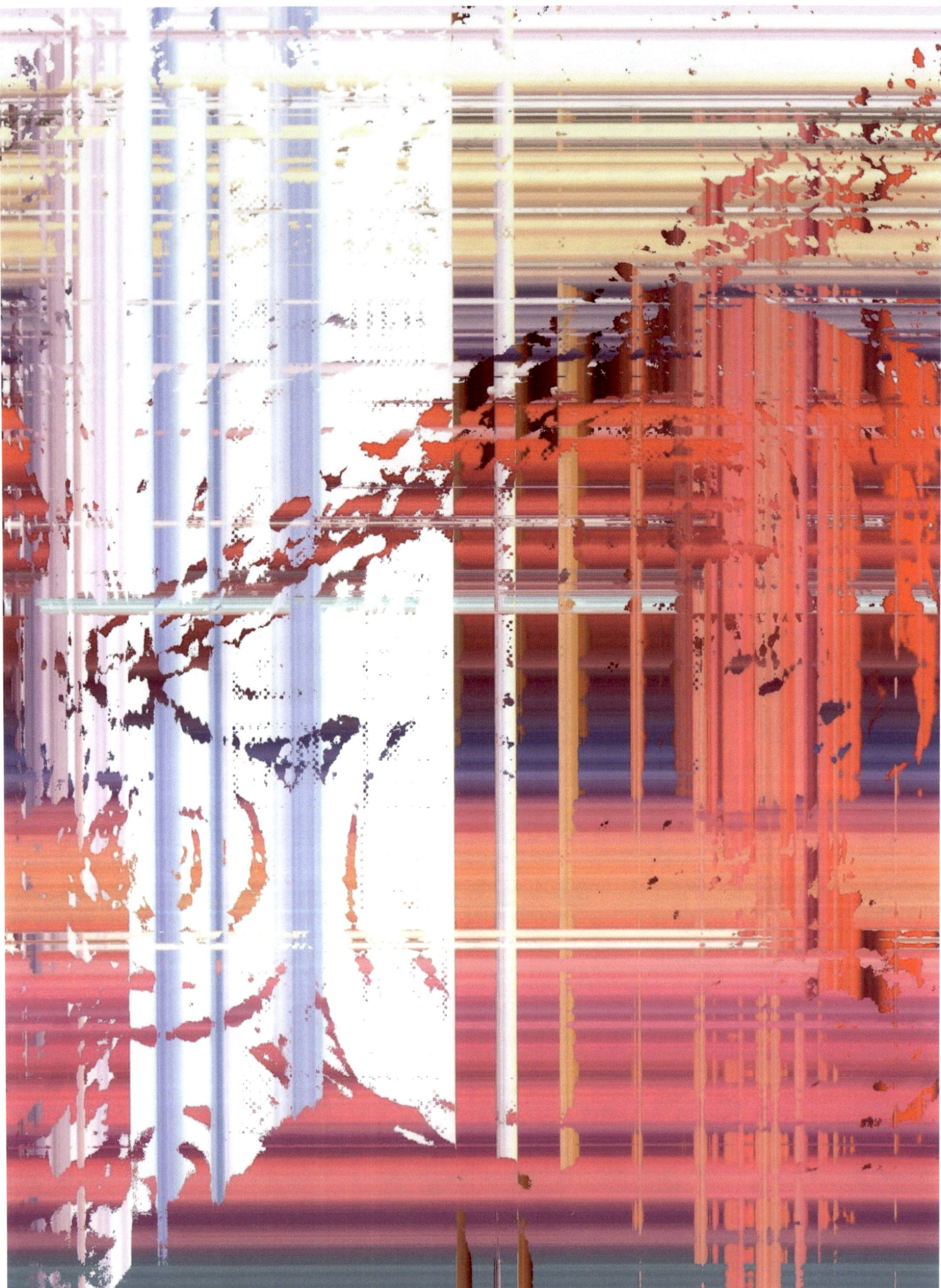

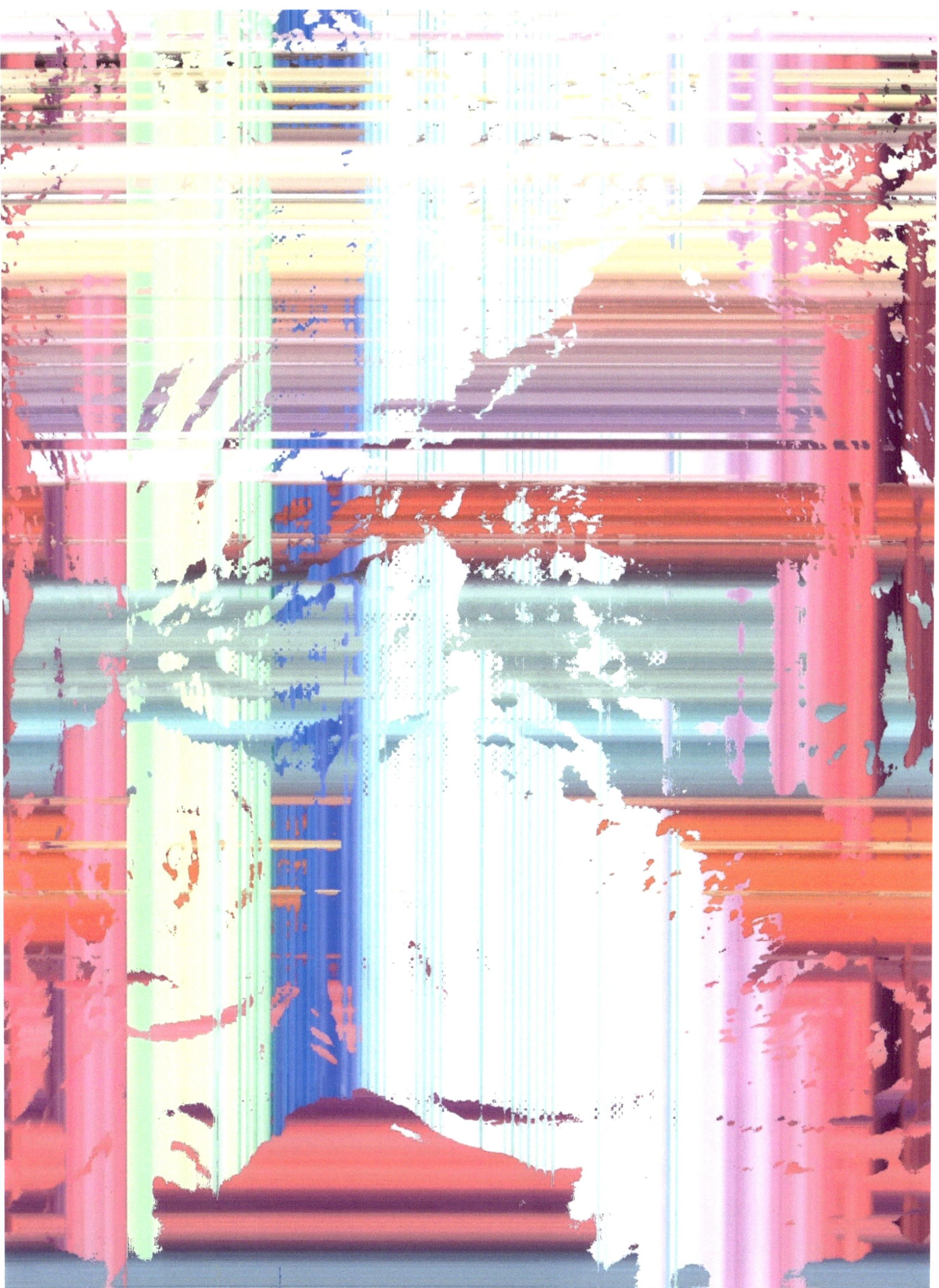

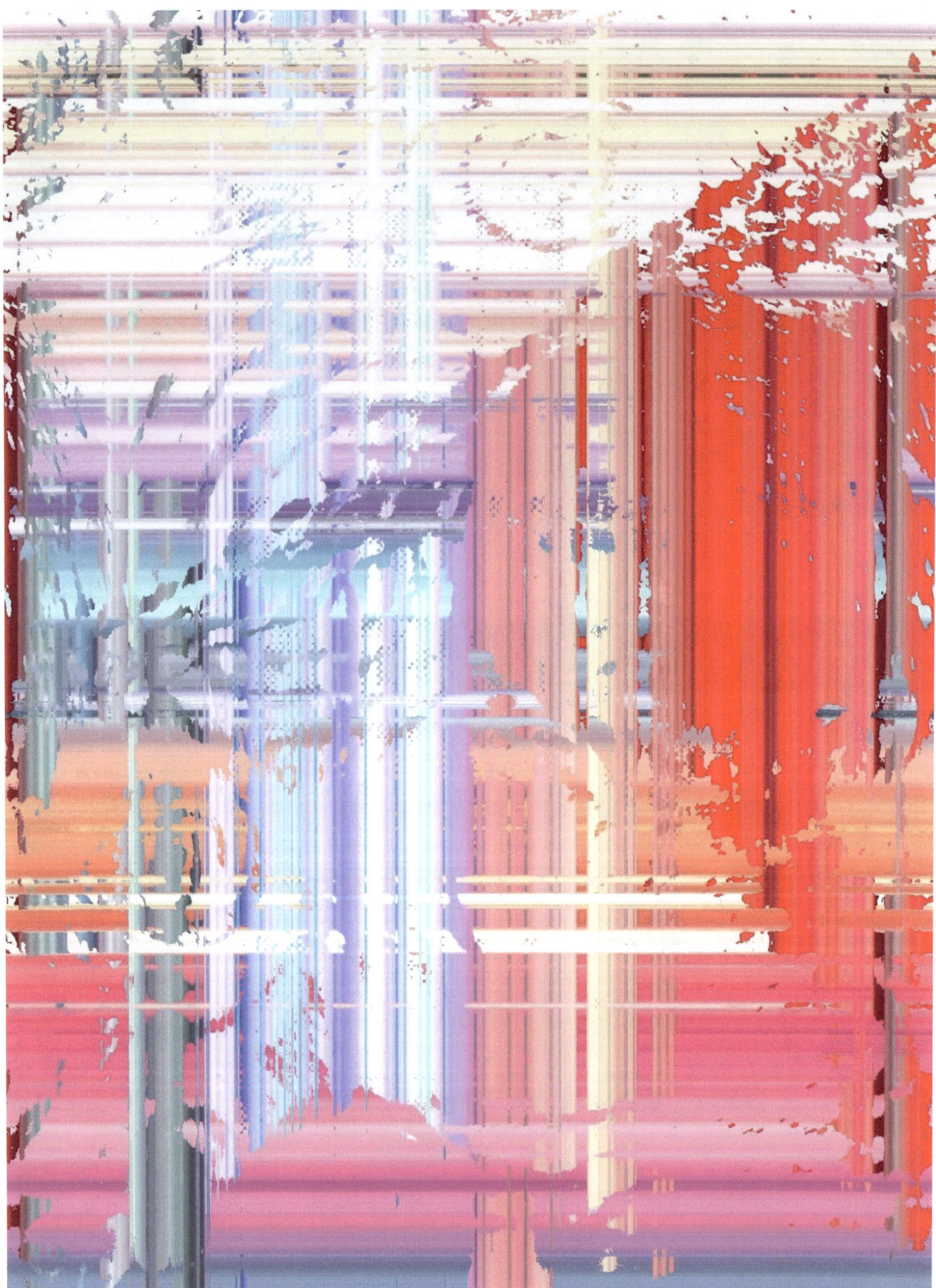

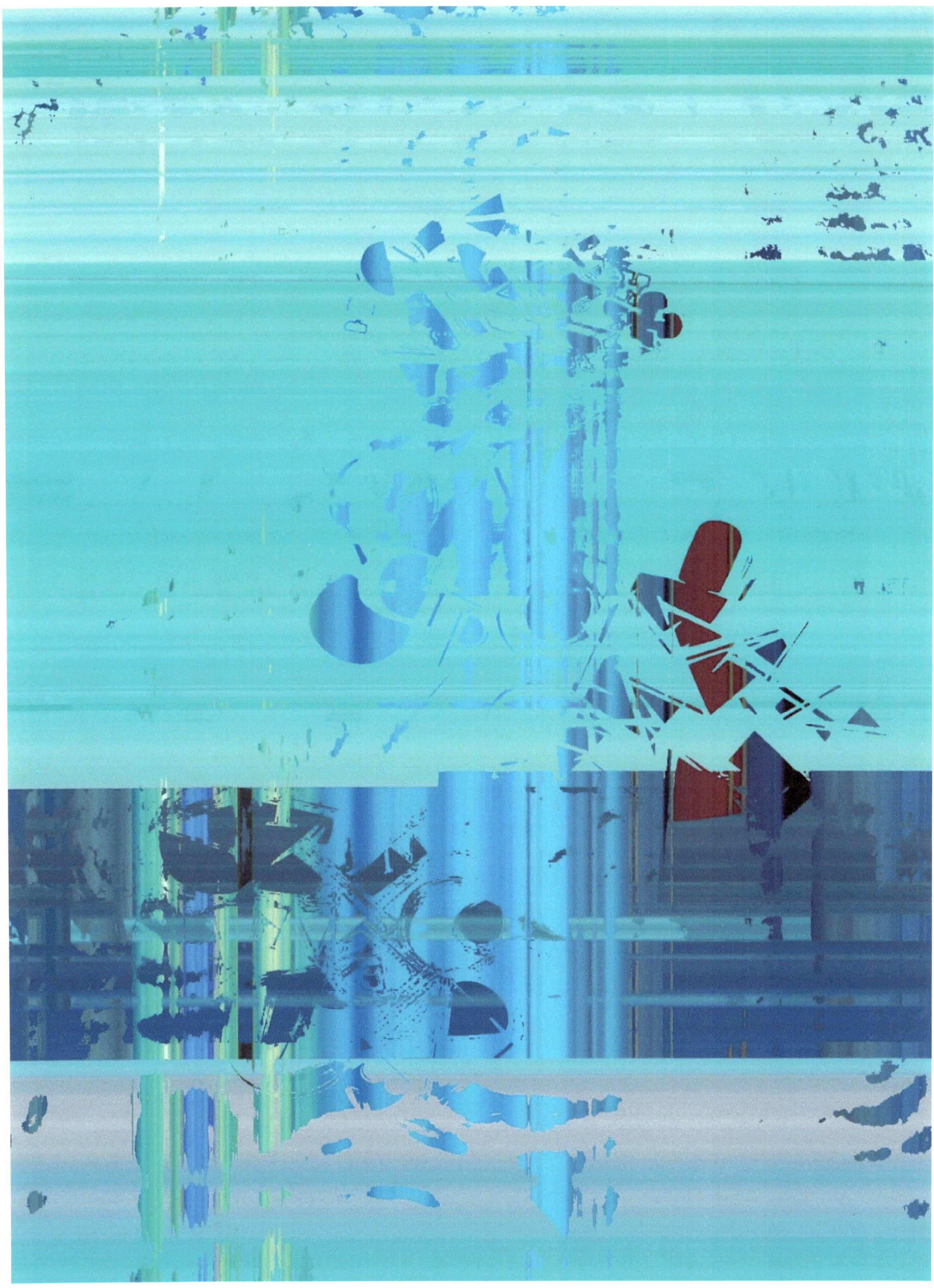

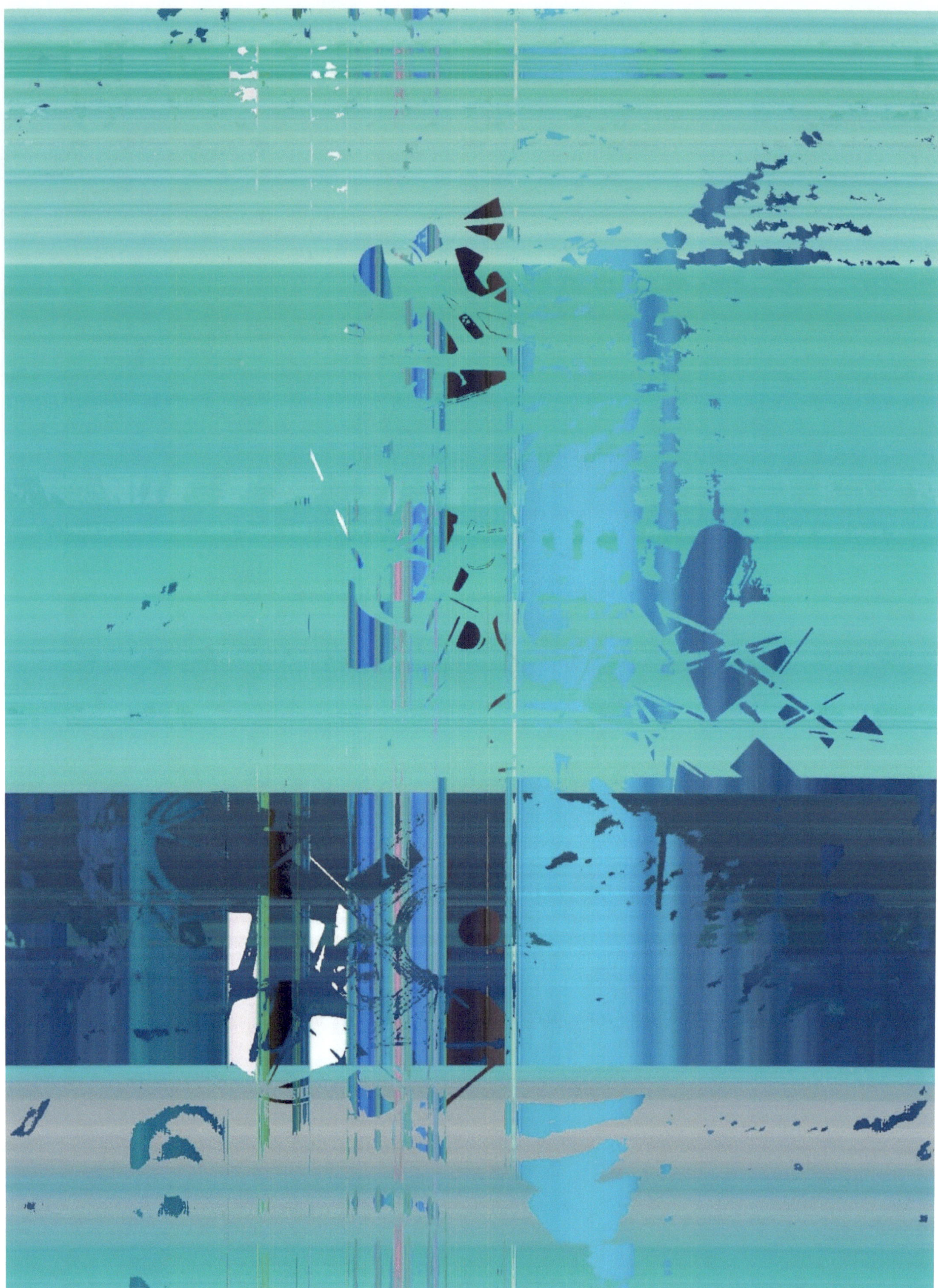

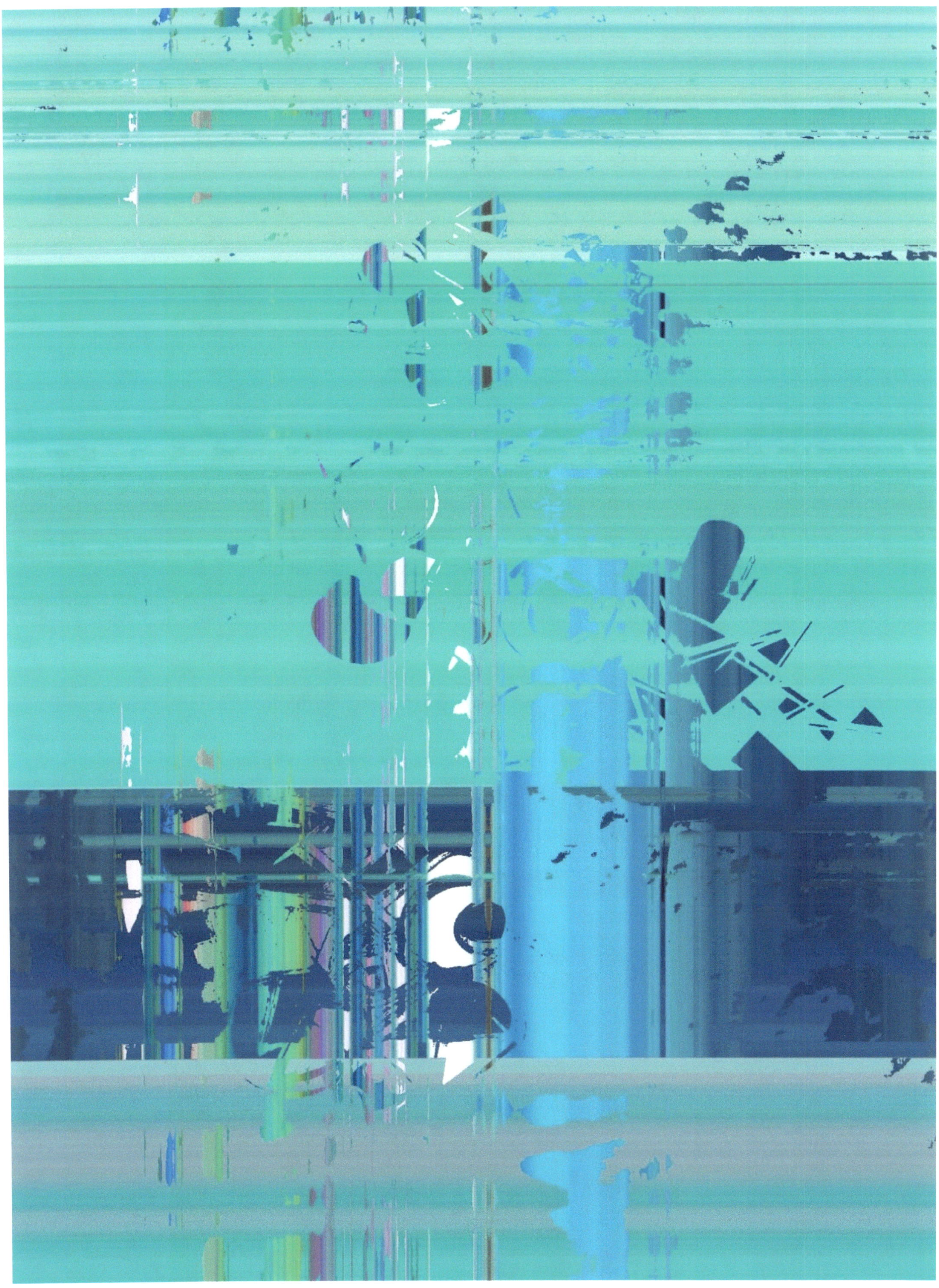

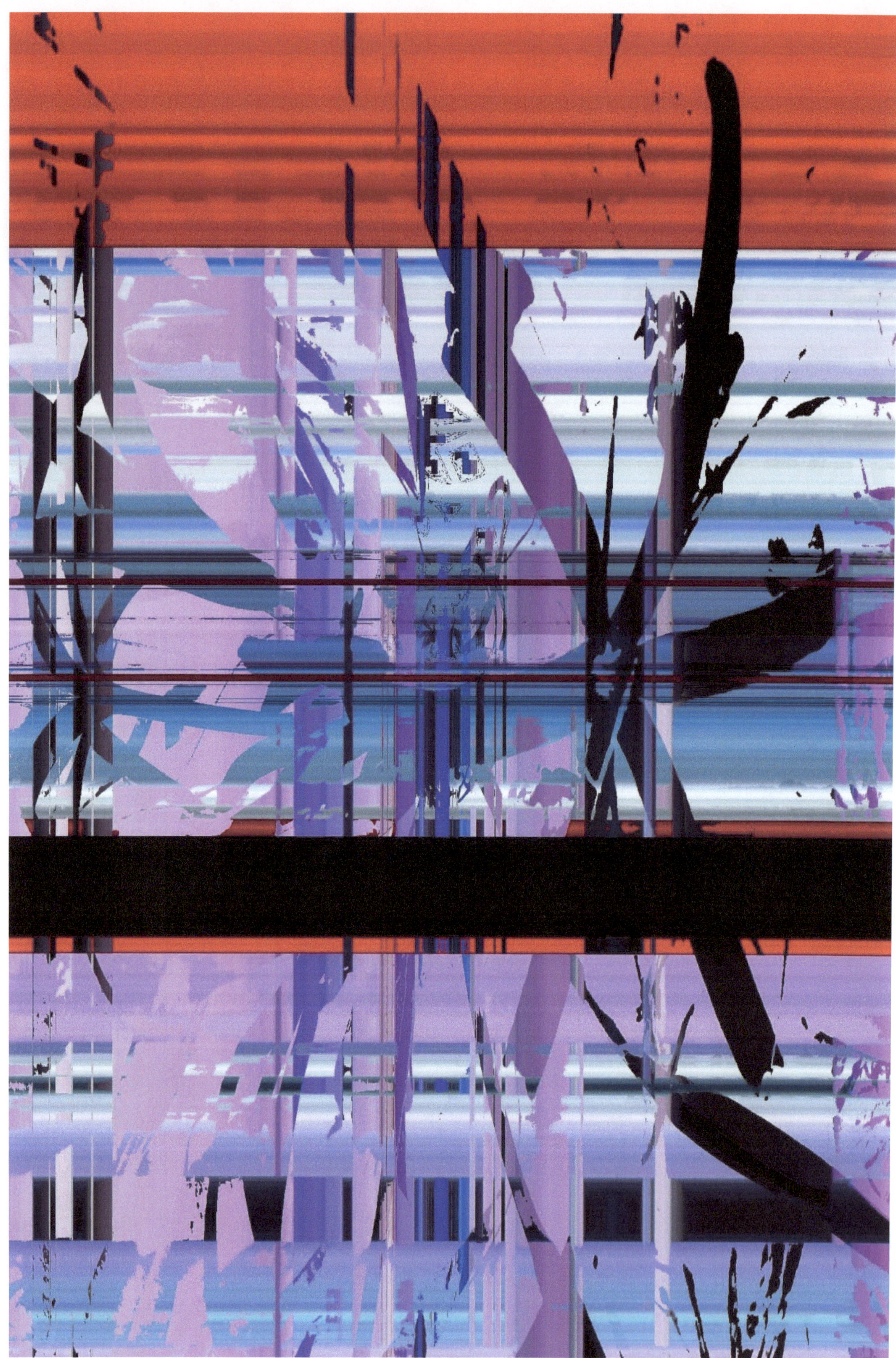

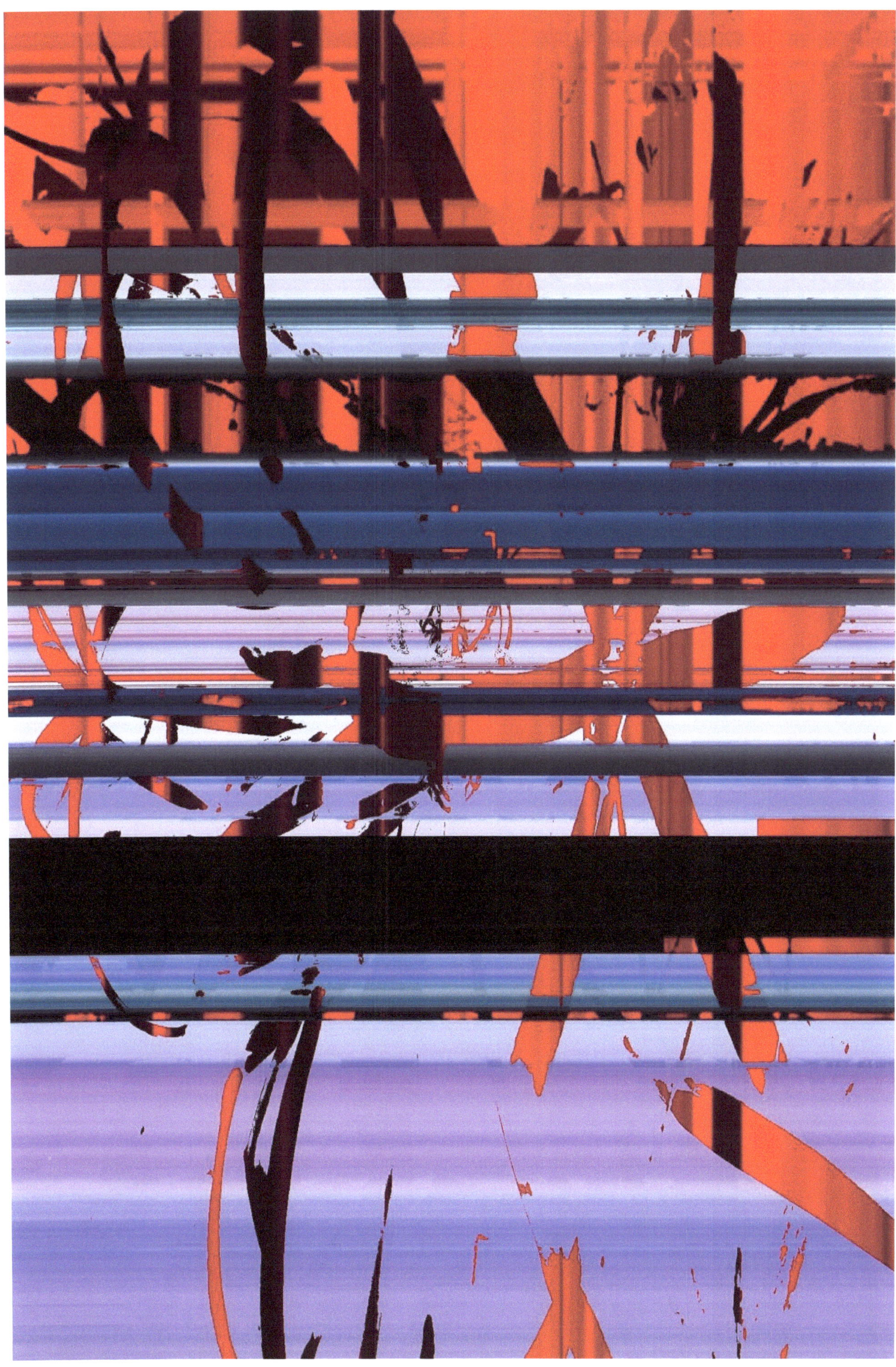

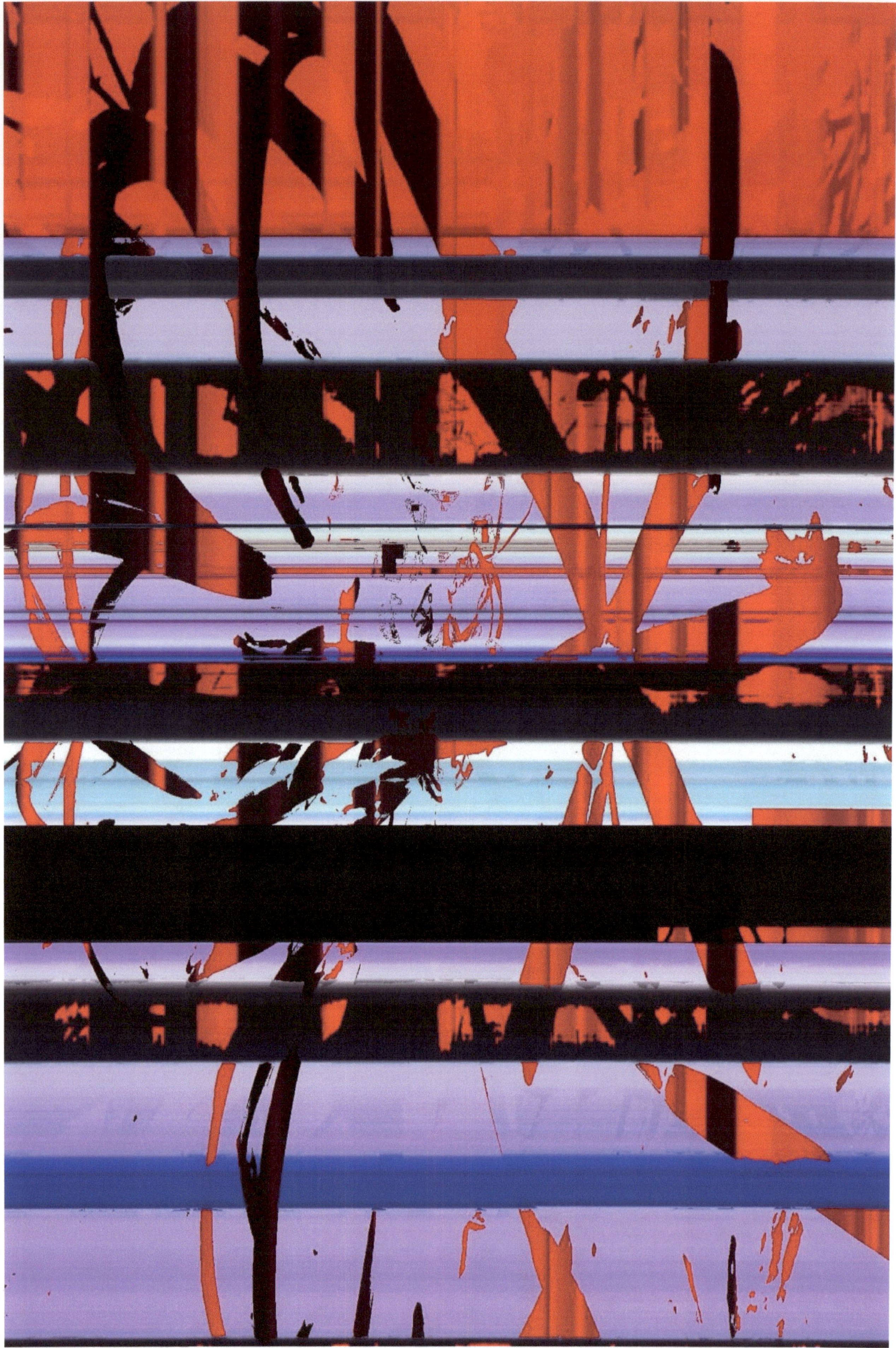

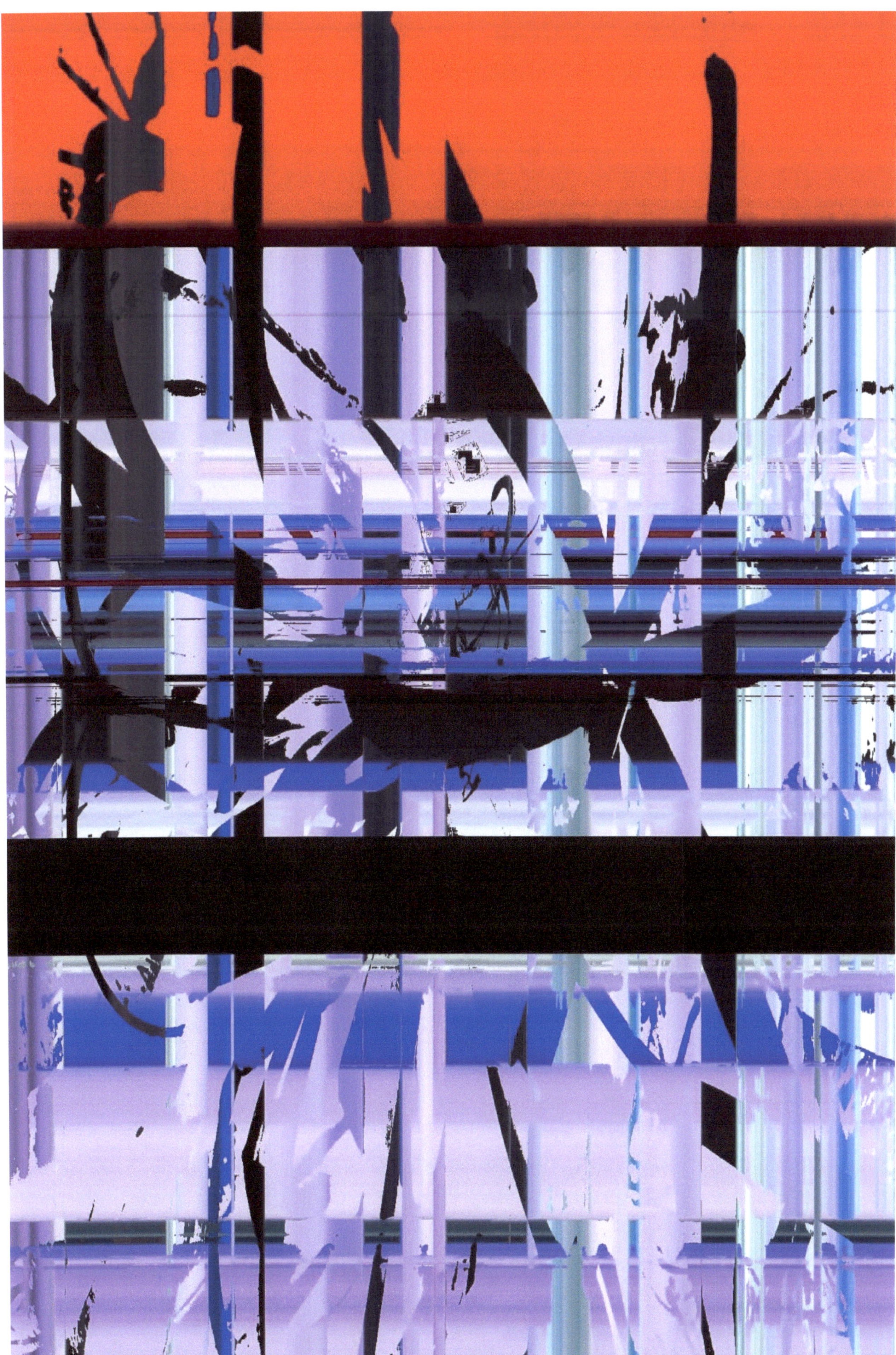

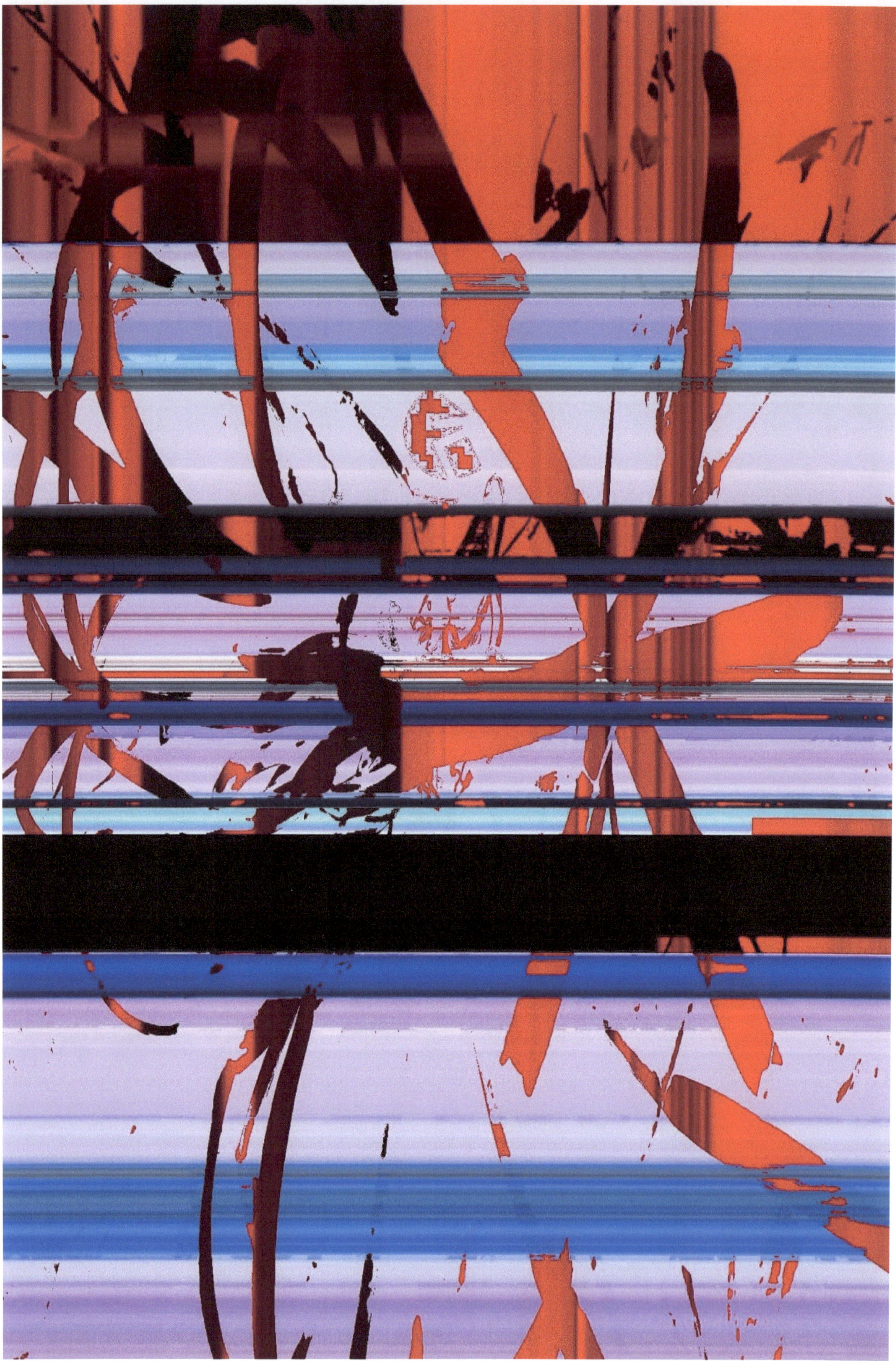

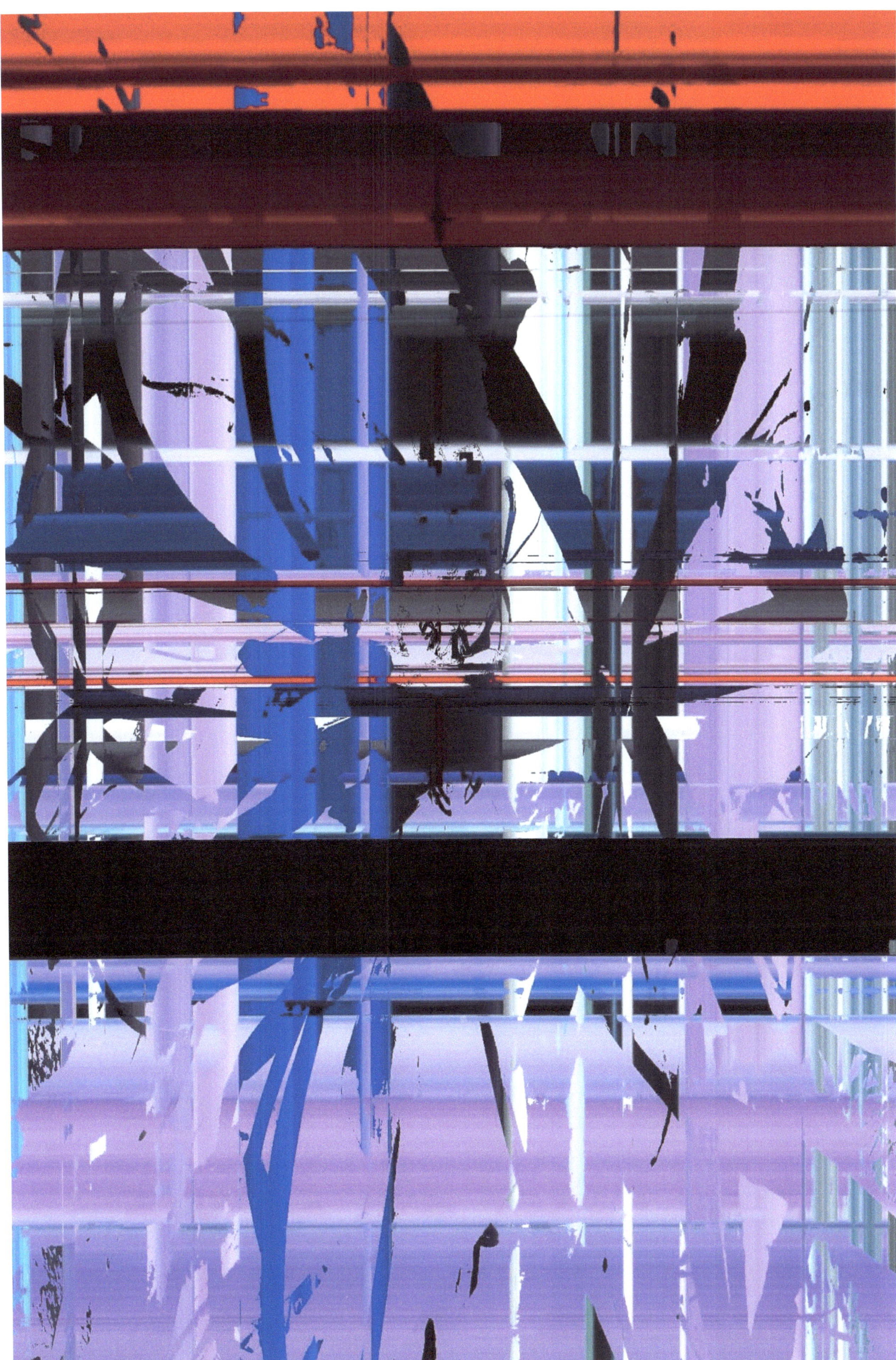

Immediately upon entering NEON GALAX by Kristine Snodgrass & Andrew Brenza I find myself asking, can I make constellations here? And, if I can, should I? The answers seem clear: yes, of course I can make constellations here. Here, and almost everywhere else. And no, that's not what this is for. Don't do it.

Should I nevertheless recall Eugen Gomringer's early statement on concrete poetry? "In the constellation something is brought into the world. It is a reality in itself and not a poem about something or other. The constellation is an invitation." From Line to Constellation (1954) Eugen Gomringer, published in Concrete Poetry: A World View, (1968, Indiana University Press) (available online at UBUWEB) I cannot refuse to consider it.

Four pages into the book, I am asked to consider letters without words. An architecture appears, an arcology. I think of the work of Nico Vassilakis, residing as it does somewhere between the concrete and the asemic, a cosmos or perhaps a galaxy of letters detached from their words. (In an email to me Kristine says of her glitched versions of Andrew's works: "They seem like little galaxies.")

I am reminded of Crag Hill's introduction to Alphabet Noir, by Vassalakis: "The letter is not the building block. The letter is a building itself, the process of meaning processing the language building meaning."

In NEON GALAX we encounter letterforms oriented in all directions, fragments of familiar typographical shapes, with no sign of handwriting anywhere. Partially through the book, the architectural structure disappears and the sense of letter-fragments drifting in interstellar space begins to assert itself. After six pages of that we find a series of abstract windows, followed by a series of oceanic images. In the final five pages of the book the glitched letter-forms fragment into an abstract dystopia, as if we are now looking out through the broken windows of the earlier architectural structures.

NEON GALAX is a very beautiful book, but don't expect all sweetness and light when you enter its world. There are jagged edges everywhere you look. Everything is broken. Kristine Snodgrass & Andrew Brenza have given us a book we might be forced to reckon with by using the term post-asemic. We might imagine a path, from concrete poetry, through varieties of visual poetry and experimental textual poetry, then to and through at least one thread of asemic writing, and now into the post-asemic, where residues of description and expressivity begin to reappear in the writing. But it is not the kind of description we all remember, nor is it a familiar sort of expressivity. Things have changed, and the story of the changes is no longer offered as a story.

—Jim Leftwich

Andrew Brenza's recent chapbooks include *Geometric Mantra* (above/ground press), *Poems in C* (Viktlösheten Press), and *Waterlight* (Simulacrum Press). He is also the author of four collections of visual poetry, *Automatic Souls* (Timglaset), *Gossamer Lid* (Trembling Pillow Press), *Alphabeticon & Other Poems* (RedFoxPress), and *Spool* (Unsolicited Press). His newest book, *Smear*, was just released from BlazeVOX Books.

Kristine is the author most recently of *Rank* from JackLeg Press (2021) *American Apparell* from AlienBuddha Press, *Rather,* from Contagion Press (2020) and the chapbook, *These Burning Fields* (Hysterical Books 2019) as well as *Out of the World* (Hysterical Books 2016) and *The War on Pants* (JackLeg Press 2013) which will be re-issued in the fall of 2021. Her solo poetry has appeared in *decomP*, *Versal*, *Big Bridge*, *5_Trope*, *Shampoo*, *2 River View*, *Otoliths* and *South Florida Poetry Journal* among others. She is the author of the chapbooks, *Put the Pie Away Quietly and Without Fervor* (Cy Gist Press 2012) and *Fledgling Starlet* (Grey Book Press 2009). Kristine's collaborative work with Maureen Seaton can be found in *Diode*, *Hayden's Ferry Review*, *Melusine*, *Artifice*, *LIT,* and others. Her triads with Neil de la Flor and Maureen Seaton can be found in *Guernica*, *DIAGRAM* , and the book, *Two Thieves & a Liar* (JackLeg Press 2012) and a chapbook *Facial Geometry* (Neo Pepper Press 2006). She has also collaborated with Scott Sweeney on a chapbook of poems, *Hot Body Contest* (Grey Book Press). Kristine's asemic and vispo work has been published in *Utsanga* (Italy), *Slow Forward*, *South Florida Poetry Journal, Voices de la Luna*, *Brave New Word,* and *Talking About Strawberries,* and forthing coming in *Street Cake*. She is the art editor for *SoFloPoJo*. Snodgrass has collaborated with many artists and poets. You can find some of Kristine's writing about collaboration at *TRIVIA: Voices of Feminism*. She is especially proud of her chapbook, *zero-zero*, poems in collaboration with Maureen Seaton. *Godlessness*, a book of visual and text collaborations with Collin J. Rae, was recently released from Alien Buddha Press. Collin and Kristine have many projects both published and in the works. New solo projects include: *WallPpr—vispro-tex glitches*. More at kristinesnodgrass.com.